Hannah Arendt
and the Crisis
of Israeli Democracy

Hannah Arendt
and the Crisis
of Israeli Democracy

ZOHAR MIHAELY

☙PICKWICK *Publications* · Eugene, Oregon

HANNAH ARENDT AND THE CRISIS OF ISRAELI DEMOCRACY

Pickwick Publications
An Imprint of Wipf and Stock Publishers
199 W. 8th Ave., Suite 3
Eugene, OR 97401

www.wipfandstock.com

PAPERBACK ISBN: 978-1-6667-9769-5
HARDCOVER ISBN: 978-1-6667-9768-8
EBOOK ISBN: 978-1-6667-9767-1

Cataloguing-in-Publication data:

Names: Mihaely, Zohar, author.

Title: Hannah Arendt and the crisis of Israeli democracy / Zohar Mihaely.

Description: Eugene, OR : Pickwick Publications, 2022 | Includes bibliographical references.

Identifiers: ISBN 978-1-6667-9769-5 (paperback) | ISBN 978-1-6667-9768-8 (hardcover) | ISBN 978-1-6667-9767-1 (ebook)

Subjects: LCSH: Arendt, Hannah, 1906–1975—Criticism and interpretation | Israel—Politics and government.

Classification: DS126.5 .M51 2022 (paperback) | DS126.5 .M51 (ebook)

VERSION NUMBER 101022

For my parents, Micky and Victor

I am deeply grateful to Dr. Gil Mihaely and Rev. David Pileggi for their assistance and kindness throughout the period during which this book was written.

Contents

Introduction

IN 2020, DURING THE intensification of the mass protest against Netanyahu, who then served as prime minister of Israel, several questions arose: Is this protest a revolution, and what is its chance of success? What is the legal status of the protesters? Are they rebels, rioters, or even traitors? On the other hand, protest activists claimed that the public was indifferent and not sufficiently present. Were the public's indifference and passivity due to the understanding that unprecedented violence pervaded Israeli politics, or was it a lack of understanding that the future of democracy was in danger? Simultaneously with the ongoing protests that took place in front of the prime minister's residence in Jerusalem and at intersections and bridges across the country, a deep sociopolitical crisis arose that expressed the familiar ethnic rift and the loss of trust of many citizens in government, institutions, and public service. This crisis eroded the fabric of Israeli society. It shook its foundations, partly because it was waged as a war between political blocs that replaced the representative party system and therefore abandoned the principles of debate and persuasion of political life on various real serious issues. Moreover, the sociopolitical crisis had other symptoms, such as damage to the public sphere through increasing government intervention in the economy (patterns of capital-government behavior) and the presence of the "organized lie" in politics (a strategy taken from the business world). In light of this account, the question arises: What is to be done?

In the present book, there is an attempt to think about this reality through the prism of the political theory of Hannah Arendt (1906–1975), which centers on an action that corresponds with this question, that is, with an intellectual tradition that is not satisfied with writing for itself but turns to reality to change it. According to Arendt's argument, which goes through all her writings, in the modern world, the understanding of the meaning of politics has been lost. This loss is not related to right or left or a particular economic system but to the fact that we live in a false political culture; the public sphere is saturated with prejudices inherited from a long, hegemonic, metaphysical, political thought tradition from Plato to Marx, which along with its positive aspects has led to the fact that political discourse today is now reduced to one question: Who controls whom? As if that is the essence of all human affairs.

Arendt tried to rethink politics after metaphysics and expressed it philosophically in many places and especially in the book *The Human Condition* (1958) using the existential language of Heidegger and Jaspers, through which she dislodged political action and judgment of the patterns determined by the brace of metaphysical rationalism, to re-present them with their autonomy and freedom.

For Arendt, politics has existential meaning, and it is a fundamental realm of our lives that relies on pluralism. Not on a man, but on people inhabiting the world. Hence the meaning of politics is not necessarily an activity through institutions of the political mechanism such as election campaigns for a particular position but is a space of people who settle the world and experience it in different ways. Thus, precisely in an age in which everything we were accustomed to relying upon—tradition, state institutions, public services, social consensus, party system, economic right and left—collapsed and was replaced by the rule of bureaucratic tyranny that abolished the citizen's relationship to government, Arendt's novelty is not in systematic political philosophy. But it was her ability to identify, among the tangle of forces in social reality, those with long-term consequences for the future and, above all, the distinction that the entry of people (throughout history) as a force into political space was not a momentary arbitrary disruption but marked a permanent political process.

Inspired by an ancient Greek political model recently revived in the American Revolution in the eighteenth century, Arendt brings a republican spirit of freedom and self-government, centered on developing political thinking that requires no prior knowledge but civic awareness of the potential power of our collective action. This model is built "from the bottom up," that is, from local organizations to national government in a way that distributes power among many sources who supervise each other. "Freedom" is not economic but political—the ability of citizens to act in speech and action in shared spaces in a way that matters publicly, that can be established and preserved only in group action. In other words, Arendt did not provide answers to the problems she identified, since, in her view, politics is what happens between people who are supposed to find solutions according to circumstances with which only they are familiar. She only points at the consequences of our actions to stimulate us to think in the direction we should strive for. For her, citizens are not just meant to serve as an audience for politicians's speeches and certainly not to obey prearranged orders or programs. Political action has no theoretical shortcuts like relying on the judgment of someone from the distant past (prejudice) or an ideology that presents a single interpretation of reality. A citizen of a free country is supposed to judge different situations on his own.[1]

---

1. Until her last book, Arendt wrote about the world and what people do in it. The issue of thinking's efficiency has arisen and gone unresolved from time to time. In the 1930s, she was astounded to discover that the ways of thinking she had been taught prevented intellectuals from comprehending reality: the rise of Nazism. She linked it to what she called a modern "rupture in tradition," namely that ideas and standards that we were accustomed to relying on while thinking like a "banister" have lost their credibility—such as the law that ordered murder, our sense of good and evil, authority, and so on. She realized that cognitive thinking that is unworldly in its pursuit of truth in an ideal world is unhelpful to our political endeavors. Scientific reasoning, too, casts doubt on phenomena as it seeks to uncover hidden rules underlying them. She concluded, based on Kant's distinction between *vernunft* and *verstand*, that thinking must begin with experience and seek its meaning. Because

experience flows, thinking is endless. We must "go up and down the stairs without a banister" and rely solely on our own responsibility. On the other hand, during the Eichmann trial, she witnessed a man who only acted without thinking, prompting her to question whether thinking can prevent evil in the world. Her premise was that there are no "dangerous thoughts," but thinking itself is dangerous because it can undermine our faith and identity. As a result, evil is to be found in the process of thinking itself. And she devoted her final unfinished book, *The Life of the Mind*, to this investigation. It begins with an unusual question: What happens when we do nothing but think? Where are we when we think? Arendt divides the thought process into two parts. We encounter something in the world, pause, and retreat to a private space where we evoke images of that experience in our imagination and reflect on them. However, because we live in a physical world in which everything that appears is meant to be seen and heard, which is the human pluralistic condition of politics, how can an invisible mental activity dealing with invisible thoughts matter in it? Metaphor, according to Arendt, bridges the gap between the physical and mental worlds. We think with words, and language has a metaphorical foundation. Metaphors emerge from the real world. And this keeps us connected to the world even when we withdraw from it to think. We remain in the world physically, but mentally we are in what Arendt calls a gap "between past and future" into which we retreat. Against the singularity of an illusory autonomic thinking-ego of Platonic-Cartesian dualism, we remain connected to others through common sense, which allows us to discover what we share and build a political body. Kant called it "extended thinking" (*erweitere Denkungsart*), in which everyone tests his opinion against other people's opinions, and thus we become "citizens of the world." As a result, thinking indirectly acts in the world through rational speech to other people about the meaning of our experience, while each individual thinks before acting in the world, thereby preventing evil. Plato's *Gorgias* provided the formulation for Arendt's twofold process: thinking is a quiet dialogue of man with himself, "two-in-one" (Greek: *eme emautō*). Socrates stated that it was "better for him to be at odds with the entire world than to contradict himself" (Plato, *Dialogues*, 1:269–70). As a result, he caused people to pause and consider whether they truly believe what they say. In fact, most of the time, thinking is useless. That is why people do not engage in it. This halt and retreat is an annoyance. Thus, it is a battle with common sense for all of us, not just philosophers. However, disruption and war with the world are advantageous in dark times when the masses are swept away by demagogue slogans and only a minority accustomed to critical thinking stops and judges common sense, thus making thinking visible in the world. The crowd looks at them and begins to wonder, perhaps even think. According to Arendt, "judging" (critical reflexive thinking, self-responsibility) is thus the mental activity best suited to post-metaphysical politics because it encounters a concrete reality without the need for a cognitive or even moral "banister" (knowledge), but rather practice. Contrary to the rule of a minority

From the broad Arendtian corpus, I have chosen to focus on *Crises of the Republic* (1971), which is recommended for those who encounter her work for the first time or those interested in politics. The articles in it open up to the reader the possibility of watching Arendt think about the world, about politics, and the way she tries to apply her methods of thinking and analysis from her great works in dealing with the issues that were at stake while she was writing. In a sense, *Crises of the Republic* is the second volume of her earlier book *Between Past and Future* (1961), which was comprised of eight articles (in the second edition) that she called "exercises in thinking about politics." A particularly important connection is found between the article "Lying in Politics" that accompanies the article "Truth and Politics" published in the second edition of *Between Past and Future*. The articles in *Between Past and Future* are important and brilliant but still a bit philosophical, like the book *The Human Condition*, and may be difficult for someone who enters Arendt's thought for the first time without a background in philosophical training. The articles in *Crises of the Republic*, on the other hand, are more understandable because they were written in response to events that took place at the time of the writing (especially in America in the late sixties and early seventies), and they do not engage in historical analysis as there is in her books *Origins of Totalitarianism* or in *Eichmann in Jerusalem*, nor do they engage in abstract analysis as in her book *The Human Condition*.

---

of experts in the Platonic tradition, we all share this faculty of "judging." It has two metrics. First, being consistent with yourself entails avoiding murder, not because the law requires it but because such an act disrupts our inner ballance (Plato). Even if good people sometimes enjoy bad things, they cannot live with a murderer. Second, Arendt refined Kant's observation that aesthetic judgment also applies to politics. Political judgment, like artistic evaluation, is not scientific. However, taste is not solely subjective; it is also related to correctness. We must try to persuade those who think Hitler was a great leader that this is a bad decision. Arendt demonstrated in the 1960s that, while thinking occurs outside of the world, it is necessary for political action. She admired the student protesters, but she believed they failed because they did not think enough and were caught up in tired old slogans from Marx and others, rather than creating a new common sense that would help them enlist people to help their revolution succeed.

The subject of the first article is the American strategy in the Vietnam War. The second article is about clarifying the concept of "civil disobedience" in the sixties. And in the third article, Arendt discusses the phenomenon of glorification of violence and why it became a problem, an ideology, and a need from the end of the twentieth century and the beginning of the twenty-first century. The fourth article, "Thoughts on Politics and Revolution" is an adaptation of one of her late interviews, driven by her worries and reactions to the uneasiness of the sixties. In this book, I will present the main arguments of the articles and discuss them in general, as well as look through them at important aspects of Israel's political reality today, as reflected in the anti-Netanyahu protests that were an everyday occurrence. This is in an attempt to formulate current insights that help explain this reality and the challenges it faces, demonstrating that Arendt spoke from her time to our time and is essential for today's public sphere discourse in Israeli democracy.

CHAPTER 1

The Essentials
of Arendt's Political Theory

THIS CHAPTER AIMS TO introduce the reader to the framework of
Arendtian political thought, which she developed—since her early
essays—from a maximal philosophical-historical perspective from
which she formulated the meaning of politics, namely the principles that became so identified with her, to distinguish between
genuine politics and that which destroys it.

Arendt speaks of two beginnings of the Western tradition
of political thought. First, there is an ancient political experience documented in the Homeric poetry expressed in the term
isonomia in which people gathered in the public sphere and took
part in self-government: all rule together, in which the concept of
command and obedience does not exist. Arendt calls this tradition
"Socratic" because Socrates did not enter the public sphere to communicate some absolute truth, that is, to control, but viewed political activity as based on pluralism of opinions. Coercion and giving
orders instead of nonviolent persuasion through speech were seen
as pre-political, typical of the hierarchies in the household in the
polis and the barbaric life outside it. This political experience un-
derwent a serious crisis with the death of Socrates: people did not
accept his speech and persuasion, and he was executed according
to the majority opinions. Due to this, Plato doubted persuasion

in speech and opinion and placed against it the philosophical truth. Because debates with the truth (in the marketplace) reduced truth to a random opinion, a minority of experts must impose the truth—which only they are capable of achieving—upon the masses by force and violence.

Thus began, according to Arendt, the second Greek tradition: the Platonic—passed down to us by the Romans—and continued as far as Marx. On the ground of the division between body and mind, Plato saw the philosopher—as the only one who could control his body—as the ultimate model for a governor. The idea of the philosopher-king, a tradition in which political action was divided into order givers ("those who know") and obedients (everyone else), led to a rationale of utilitarianism, governing controlled by moral standards ("yardsticks"), namely a system that freezes the citizens' initiative inherent in the human nature. Scholastic Christianity continued the exclusion of (political) action by turning its back on this world. At the same time, it contributed to the principles of forgiveness and promise that (according to Arendt) belong to genuine politics.

Due to what Arendt views as a modern rupture of tradition (which despite its flaws also helped preserve a common world despite generational change) and the "rise of the social" in the French Revolution and Marxism (which spawned the consumer mass society that elevated the necessity of work at the expense of the spontaneous political action of Homeric experience) the public sphere, which was meant for exercising freedom through political action, was conquered by necessary work (the production-consumption cycle does not leave room for spontaneous actions). Ultimately, this led to a situation where the political question of forming a government (the relation between government and the people) became a matter of "foreign affairs," as if a government is needed only to negotiate with other countries. In other words, the public sphere is filled with prejudices—"empty shells," that is, concepts whose original meaning was forgotten and distorted by the imagination. Sovereign rule, relations of control and obedience necessary for bad politics are the only things left today, to which was added in the nuclear age a new prejudice, namely that it is desirable to remove politics—which monopolized the means of violence—from our lives once and for all.

At the heart of Arendt's thought is, therefore, a project of deconstructing Platonic tradition as far as Marx, like plucking pearls from seashells—removing motifs of control while extracting genuine motifs to bring them together, to restore the older Homeric revolutionary tradition and build from it a new post-metaphysical political thinking based on a horizontal form of government and participatory democracy, that is, an idea of politics without imperative attitude and obedience. For this reason, Arendt was excited about the American Revolution, finding in it manifestations of revolutionary attempts that conform to the first Greek political tradition—namely the adoration of greatness (Homeric), action as the foundation of a new beginning (Roman), and the ability to keep promises and act as forgiveness (Christian). In her view, the importance of the American Revolution was mainly expressed in alliances and conventions created by political bodies that did not function as governments but as political communities that created a common political domain with the power capable of claiming rights but not claiming sovereignty. In the American Revolution, the question of the form of government was finally asked: it was not just an uprising against the government as in the French Revolution but against the very idea of control and obedience, and the founding of a new beginning (*novus ordo saeclorum*), although her book *On Revolution* concludes that this revolutionary spirit of the founding fathers of the United States was forgotten shortly after the founding of the republic.

CHAPTER 2

Lying in Modern Politics

THE ESSAY "LYING IN Politics" deals with Arendt's analysis of the Pentagon Papers. For her, these documents are a case study of a new kind of political lie. While traditionally lying in politics was aimed at the enemy, it is now aimed at the people and Congress, namely: self-deception. America did not open war in self-defense or for some geopolitical reason such as making a profit by occupying territory but to create an image in world public opinion, especially among the Soviets, according to which the United States is the number one power in the world. And this "organized lie," spread by top officials with an old-school Cold War-era anti-communist ideology and "problem-solving" experts from a social science academic background who were hired to help them make decisions, formed the infrastructure of American domestic and foreign policy during a decade.

Arendt first presents the theoretical background of the phenomenon of lying in politics she mentioned earlier in the article "Truth and Politics"—to which lies and political action are linked. Truth has never been a value in politics. Secrecy and mystery of an administration, fabrications, and lies have always been seen as legitimate tools for the conduct of statesmen, and, surprisingly, this hasn't been prioritized in the political thought tradition. In Arendt's theory, the nature of political action is the beginning of something new, not necessarily out of nothing. Sometimes, to allow space for action, it is necessary to move an existing thing or change it. In politics, such a change is possible only if the actor imagines himself somewhere other than what exists. To get there, he must lie about the world. For example, Martin Luther King Jr. spoke about a world in which skin color does not matter. Of course, it is a lie, but the ability to lie, to deny facts, has to do with the ability to act politically, because the root of both is the imagination. Action—the substance from which politics is made—is impossible without this freedom. Thus, when talking about the lies of political actors it is important to remember that the lie did not sneak into politics by chance or sin, and therefore moral rage will not make it go away. Herein lies in a sense the provocativeness of the article—real political action requires lying.

THE ADVANTAGE OF THE LIAR

Arendt explains that facts need credible testimony to establish themselves safely in the field of human affairs. That is, no fact cannot be undermined because of its contingency: seemingly, there is always a possibility that it was otherwise. This fragility makes the lie so easy and tempting. Hence the liar's advantage is in that the fact is not in conflict with logic; things can also be as the liar presents them. Moreover, lies are often more logical, and thus more preferable, because they are planned and arranged, in contrast to the surprise factor of reality itself.

ATTACK AGAINST REALITY

According to Arendt, even though politics is—in a sense—about lying, the danger is not the image that we are in a better place elsewhere but that the excessive lying can lead to the loss of any truth and the stabilizing fact that we share a common world, which she calls "the earth under our feet."[1] There is a point where the public loses the ability to distinguish between truth and falsehood to survive. In fact, we lie in order to survive. However, over time, a public

1 Arendt, *Between Past and Future*, 253.

that has lost the sense between truth and imagination begins to rebel. And under normal circumstances, the lie will be defeated by reality. The experience of totalitarian regimes has taught that despite dictators' belief in the power of lies—for example, rewriting history to keep up with the current political line or obscuring information incompatible with ideology—as in a socialist economy, the regime has denied unemployment and the unemployed have become invisible—the lies will last only a short time, for example, by terrorism and violence. Even if they cover the world with lies, there will always be a library somewhere where data that they tried to hide remains.

In the main part of the article, Arendt provides a detailed account of the forces operating within the campaign structure of the Vietnam War. On one side of the barricade is the intelligence community, which represents the factual truth. On the other hand, the "ideologists"—that is, the president and his senior advisers, whether intentionally or out of self-lie or a strange combination of the two, express ideology. And there are the people in the middle, the problem-solvers, and the public relations people who work for the ideologist, and know that they are lying, and yet they somehow justify the lie and become the civilized face of the government.

Turning a fact into an opinion requires a new form of falsehood. In addition to totalitarian attempts to rewrite history, Arendt claims new modern types of political lying have emerged:

1. Publicity Tactics

For the most part, governments' policies today are not designed to make people's lives better, but to establish images of producing better lives. That is, what matters is the image and not the facts. Arendt assumes that this has something to do with public relations and the idea that the Vietnam War was perceived as an image. The goal was not to win in order to conquer a piece of land but to preserve the U.S. image as an ultimate world power and loyal ally. To this end, the government hired public relations managers (communications consultants, speechwriters, etc.), whose mentality and tactics were taken from the business world and the consumer society. Their job was to create for politicians public images detached from reality. Since, contrary to politicians, they were subjected to a reality that sets limits to their imagination, they used the stick-and-carrot method (incentives and punishments). That is, they manipulated the mind of the "consumer." In Arendt's words: "The goal now is the image itself . . . and the creators of the image think that manipulation controls the minds of people, and hence that it is what controls the world."[2] If you make people think that the government is functioning well, that you are helping the economy, and that you won the war—it's better than making things better in reality. Arendt points out that ironically the president of the United States is prone to fall into manipulations more than others. Due to his complex role, he is surrounded by consultants and managers who practice their power through filtering the information and interpretation of the outside world they provide to him. Thus the position of the most powerful man in the most powerful state is predefined.

From the idea of public relations, Arendt continues to a more provocative idea, which is less commonly encountered in everyday life but plays an important role in Pentagon documents:

2. Problem-Solvers

A nickname for a group of military personnel and civil servants who have been recruited to the government from universities, usually from the social sciences. A large portion of the authors of the Pentagon documents belonged to this group. They are equipped— in their opinion and the opinion of their superiors—with theories and methods of analysis that have prepared them to "solve all the problems of foreign policy." They are characterized by excessive self-confidence and have worked in front of military personnel who are used to winning. In retrospect, it can be said that their integrity enabled the writing of the Pentagon papers. They may have been patriots by accident, but they did not lie to ensure the state's

2. Arendt, *Crises of the Republic*, 20.

survival. The U.S. was not in existential danger vis-à-vis North Vietnam. Although they were intelligent professional intellectuals, they also believed that politics is a form of public relations. The difference between them and regular PR people is that they were also problem-solvers.

They were not naive; some doubted the government's commitment to the war.

But they believed in methods and not in worldviews. They were proud of their rationality and were eager for theories, a mental effort to explain the world. They longed for pseudo-mathematical formulas that could connect seemingly disparate phenomena in reality, eager to discover laws that would allow them to predict political and historical facts as if they were as necessary and credible as natural phenomena that a physicist observes. Yet the problem-solvers lacked the patience of natural scientists to wait for verification or refutation of their theses by facts. Instead, they adapted the "reality"—which was invented by them anyway and could therefore also be different—to their theories, and thus they eliminated the disturbing fragility of these theories. Most of these theory games, aimed at an imaginary audience, were based on averages: a middle ground between two extreme possibilities, in a way that leads to human insensitivity. They said, for example, that "if we bombed North Vietnam it would raise the morale in South Vietnam. We are not sure, but maybe it will work."

3. Ideologists

Not only had the problem-solvers lost their heads because they relied on the power of calculation and not on the human ability to learn from reality, but the Cold War ideologists preceded them. It was not the old anti-communism (American hostility to socialism) from the 1920s, which remained the mainstay of the Republican Party in Roosevelt's time, but a new anti-communism, an ideology that had been at the root of all theories in Washington since the end of World War II. The central thesis of this ideology was "the domino theory," according to which if South Vietnam fell to the North, all other Southeast Asian countries would fall into the arms of communism. Ignoring relevant facts and neglecting post-World War II developments have become the hallmark of the establishment's doctrine. The ideologists did not need facts, information, because they had a theory that any fact that did not match it was denied. Unlike Robert McNamara's young team, the "ideologists" were less complex or intellectual than the problem-solvers but no less effective in segregating people from the effects of reality and destroying judgment and learning ability. They boasted that they had learned from the past—from Stalin's rule over the Communist Parties (hence the conception of monolithic communism) and Hitler's opening of the war after the Munich Conference—that any gesture of reconciliation is a "second Munich" ploy, that is, "if we do not stop the Nazi march, they will destroy the world." They were unable to deal with reality according to its rules and always had parallels in their head that "helped" them understand it.

Common to problem-solvers and liar politicians is the confidence in de-factualization, the confidence that it is possible to get rid of facts, due to their contingency. The problem is that facts do not disappear just because a particular public believes they do not exist. Therefore this approach requires destruction. In the article "Truth and Politics," Arendt argues that "organized lying" always tends to destroy what the liar comes to deny, although only the totalitarian regime took the lie as the first step before the murder. When Trotsky learned that he had not played a role in the revolution in Soviet books, he knew there was a contract on his head. But as mentioned, even in the case of Stalin, where both will and belief in omnipotent power were mobilized in favor of de-factualization, there is still no ability to omit Trotsky's name from all the archives in all libraries in the world.

Problem-solvers and politicians treat hypotheses as well-founded facts. Arendt cites as an example the theory of Walt Rostow, the dominant intellectual in the Johnson administration, which became the central rationale in the decision to bomb North Vietnam—against McNamara's prestigious systematic analysis.[3] Rostow's theory actually relied on an incidental remark by one

3. See Stavins et al., *Washington Plans Aggressive War*, 212.

of the sharpest and most up-to-date observers among war crit-ics, Bernard Fall, that North Vietnamese President Ho Chi Minh might deny war in the South if one of his new industrial plants served as a target. This remark was in line with Rostow's theory of guerrilla warfare and was therefore changed to a fact: the North Korean president has an industrial compound he seeks to protect, hence he is not a guerrilla fighter who has nothing to lose. In ret-rospect, this seems to have been a misjudgment—North Vietnam was revealed as a nonindustrialized country. But that was enough to justify an enormous American airstrike on the North, which resulted in the deaths of a large number of civilians. All this was in the context of a "limited war."

And finally, in this "Alice in Wonderland" atmosphere, there was one group left with their feet on the ground.

THE INTELLIGENCE COMMUNITY

Arendt distinguishes the problem-solvers and PR people from the intelligence community, who were independent and therefore con-sistently provided reliable information throughout the war. While problem-solvers and military personnel focused on ideologies or theories and hypotheses, Arendt was under the impression that the intelligence community had stepped back and carried out its role, putting the facts on the table. They did not have to present positive results and they were not under pressure from Washington to pro-duce good news, for example, to concoct legends about "continued progress." The price of this objectivity was the ineffectiveness of their reports on National Security Council decision-making. On the other hand, Arendt was also impressed that the problem-solvers—those intellectuals from the universities—raped the ac-curate reports of the intelligence community to fit the ideologies and goals set by the politicians. Taking the "domino theory" as an example, the CIA assessed that, except for Cambodia, no country seemed to have succumbed to communism following the fall of Laos and the south. According to the Pentagon Papers, although only two—Rostow and General Taylor—accepted the domino thesis literally, everyone else continued to use it as a working assumption for everything, and in fact, saw it as a "fact."

Arendt is basically trying to answer Daniel Ellsberg's question—"How could they do that?" Why, in a democracy like the U.S. in the sixties, can a group of government officials lie so consistently? Why would a country that emerged from World War II as the richest and most dominant power in the world like to add another small country to its customer list, or why would you like to defeat a backyard state at such a heavy price? The absurdity of investing excessive means to achieve small goals in a negligible place convinced broad sections of the American public that the establishment had lost its mind. And she offers few explanations.

First, the success of fraud. The more successful the liar, that is, the more people are convinced, the more likely he is to believe his lies. The psychological assumptions of the problem-solvers about the infinity of possibilities to manipulate people made them think that the victory "in battle" over people's minds was in their pocket. Out of this atmosphere where the fear of admitting defeat was greater than the defeat itself, all the false statements about the invasion of Cambodia were brewed. This crucial truth could only be successfully covered in the circles closest to the president—by concerns for the problem of the image of a first president who lost a war for the next election, rather than for the welfare of the American people.

Second, a liar has no better excuse than to say that his aversion to lying is so great that he had to deceive himself before others.

Third, the cold-blooded liar can afford to enjoy his prank only from the outside. In debating facts, the persuasive factor with the best chances of overcoming considerations of pleasure, fear, and profit is the personal appearance. Prejudices today tend to be harsh towards cold-blooded liars, while the developed art of self-deception usually encounters tolerance and permissiveness.

Finally, if modern political lies are so great that they require a reediting of the whole context of facts—i.e., accurate construction of a substitute context—what prevents these stories, images, and nonfacts from becoming a perfect substitute for factual reality? An "organized lie" always tends to destroy what it comes to deny. It is like when someone lies that someone died and immediately goes to kill him. And so this rationale not only created the atmosphere in the experts' work environment but also the reality outside and, finally, the insensitivity to human life. Out of a passion to turn everything into numbers and graphical curves, to provide answers according to statistical averages, the problem-solvers' reports looked like computer output. That is, they did not judge reality but engaged in calculations based on mathematical "evidence." They were not only smart but also proud of their rationality and were eager for theories, a mental effort to explain the world. They longed to find formulas in pseudo-mathematical language that would unite the most separated phenomena in reality.

BUILT-IN DE-FACTUALIZATION

The unwillingness or inability to learn from reality leads us, according to Arendt, to the heart of the question "How could they do this?"—namely how, despite all this, did they continue this absurd war until its bitter end?

She answers that de-factualization was welcomed because disregard for reality was built into policy and goals themselves. Another great ploy, secondary in importance only to the domino theory, was based on the assumption of the existence of a Soviet-Chinese bloc, in addition to a separate thesis on Chinese expansion. But when government goals in war are psychological, why do they need to understand who Indo-China is or the history and geography of the region? For example, the rift between Moscow and Peking a decade before the Chinese Revolution—a reality that was clear to anyone familiar with history who knew about the rivalry between China and Stalin, and the fragmentary nature of the communist movement since World War II—refutes the thesis of monolithic communism. And so is the fact that the Vietnamese fought invaders for 2,500 years (long before communism) and that Vietnam is not a small, primitive backyard without civilization but a nation with an ancient culture. At this point, the initial assumption that the state does not matter—which is built into domino theory—has changed to the fact that it does not matter who the enemy is at all. And all this in the middle of the war.

The left presented a counter-thesis, according to which the United States, which emerged from the war as its greatest power, began a consistent imperialist policy aimed at world domination. According to Arendt, there was no significant evidence in the Pentagon Papers of this claim. Only twice was the strategic importance of the air, sea, and land bases in the region mentioned. McNamara's 1964 report that "we have no interest in turning South Vietnam into a Western base or joining in as a member of a Western coalition,"[4] and all the American statements from that period were that the U.S. was not looking for territorial gains or any other vital gain.

Reading the Pentagon documents raises the danger of distancing oneself from reality and disregarding facts as a result of ideologizing in politics. Politicians and their aides concentrated on creating an image, but they were unaware that even its reserve could run out. They cared only about statistics—that the number of fatalities in battles is lower than the number of road accident victims in the country. Economic waste and loss of human life were justified in the name of trying to impose an image on distant peoples. The Americans had reached a point where they were not fighting communism but to prevent their humiliation. For them, they "could not lose," no matter how many casualties it took to prove this point. Considerations for the next U.S. presidential election and the international image of the United States were more important than considerations related to human life on the part of the region's natives as well as on the part of American soldiers.

Arendt concludes that as bad as the Vietnam War was, the only good thing that came out of it was the Pentagon Papers. People sat and thought about why they were going wrong. The fact that a prestigious newspaper like the *New York Times* dared to bring the material that was defined as "top secret" to the widest possible attention, along with McNamara's preparations to conduct a house-check of failures, restored the U.S. reputation, meaning all

---

4. Sheehan et al., *Pentagon Papers*, 278.

these people were reminded of their duty to the founders of the American state, a phenomenon that could occur only in the U.S. It was shown that as long as the press is free and not corrupt, it has a huge role to play and deserves to be called the "fifth branch of the government."

DISCUSSION

Even liberal democracies, as Arendt points out, are not immune to the blurring of truth and opinion, with past and present entwined in the service of government interests and ambitions, and this, too, may be coercive on the public, even in the absence of totalitarianism's brutality. As a result, how can we identify the difference between a legitimate and illegitimate lie? For example, claiming that America is the land of democracy is an intentional falsehood. It was never this way before. The most dangerous falsehood, according to Arendt, is when we not only imagine something but also strive to leave reality through mental structures and theories, and we stop seeing and hearing what is true. It is critical to state that, like America, Israel advocates for democracy, but it is equally critical not to conceal or misrepresent the fact that we are not there yet. Because we are so confident that we live in a democracy, we disregard signs of bigotry, coercion, and violence, dismissing them as minor or irrelevant. That is, we de-factualize reality, and our deception becomes an idea that we are attempting to superimpose on reality rather than an action.

What is the relevance of the respect that problem-solving professionals still enjoy in Israel today, in terms of democracy? Arendt tells us that in a democracy, experts will predict that the economy will grow or deteriorate in one way or another, that immigration will increase or decrease in one way or another, and so on. Experts, in the end, have no say in the democratic system; it is up to citizens to make such decisions. Excessive dependence on experts thus implies a rejection of the notion that people's opinions matter. People's representatives, according to Arendt, are not always expected to be experts but rather excellent at assessing right and wrong. We also need to hire folks who can make sound decisions. In this regard, unlike former Prime Minister Benjamin Netanyahu, Yair Lapid is seen as a generalist rather than a specialist, yet he has a well-developed ability to analyze. And so does the chairwoman of the Labor Party, Merav Michaeli. In the article presented here, Arendt is concerned about components of problem-solving in governments, a factor aimed to deprive individuals of their ability to make decisions. This isn't to argue that whatever people say is correct. Yet Arendt believes that people are less incorrect than bureaucrats. Experts believe their opinions are more important than regular people's and, as a result, are more likely to deceive themselves than citizens. Therefore we must be suspicious of organizations that seek to strip people of authority in the name of "truth."

Regarding de-factualization and the prospect of a totalitarian regime today, Arendt lived during the Nazi era and wrote about it as well as Stalinism, and one of the fundamental features of the totalitarian system for her was an ideology that ignored reality, that citizens were so committed to it that they simply ignored it. Arendt emphasized that the human psyche has a profound need to prefer the uniformity and coherence of theoretical truth to the chaotic complexity of factual reality. While we need imagination, ideas, and utopias to be inspired, there is a risk in merging utopias with terrorism in a way that de-factualizes the world and is driven by a single point of view. Although we now live in a world with a greater diversity of viewpoints than ever before, Arendt believes that this can be bad, since it creates insecurity. And a desire for security fosters a yearning for authoritarianism like Netanyahu's, Trump's, and Putin's, namely "a strong single man who will solve all our nuclear and climatic concerns." Or, alternatively, support for intellectuals who claim to offer a cohesive narrative that "can restore coherence to the world." From an Arendtian perspective, the task of contemporary intellectuals is to warn the public about the dangers that arise when de-factual reality becomes political.

In the Arendtian sense, the suspicion that Netanyahu purposefully ignited the (short) intifada in *Sheikh Jarrah* and the

Temple Mount to deter right-wingers from joining the "changing government" looks like public and *Knesset* (i.e., Israeli Parliament) self-deception. This went so far as to make citizens lose their ability to distinguish between picture and reality. Additional information regarding it will be disclosed during Netanyahu's current trial, despite his famous catchphrase "there will be nothing because there was nothing." For example, he has been accused of influencing media coverage of himself and his family through bribes and the appointment of right-wing people to crucial positions in popular media.

The Netanyahu administration's and its advisers' systematic attack on the canonical Zionist narrative over the years, namely the attempt to rewrite history using de-factualization agents within the educational system, has already produced a new generation of young Israeli citizens who believe that Mr. David Ben Gurion was a racist colonist who imported Jewish slaves from North African and Asian countries to feed the Ashkenazi (i.e., Jewish-Israelis of European descent) establishment. Or that former Prime Minister Rabin was a traitor rather than a war hero and statesman. As we'll see below, Arendt expanded on this in a discussion of what she considers to be another modern innovation in politics: "lying the truth," or telling the people how bad things are, that is, how rotten state institutions and infrastructures are and how they must be eliminated in their entirety. The problem is that, even if it is correct that state institutions are rotten, telling people in this way is motivated by a desire to destroy.

Finally, there is a limit to public relations. According to Arendt, people's opinions are heavily influenced by their identity, causing them to be swayed by public relations. However, there are some viewpoints that we will change. And if we never engage with other people's viewpoints, we'll never be able to participate in reality and pierce our ideological balloon, or the coherent story we tell ourselves. Meeting people from outside your cocoon has something, if not all, of an impact.

CHAPTER 3

Civil Disobedience in the 1960s and Its Significance Today

THIS ARTICLE INVESTIGATES THE phenomenon of civil disobedience in anti-Vietnam War movements, Arendt's most obvious democratic manifesto. The background for the article, which runs from here to the end of her book *Crises of the Republic*, is Arendt's claim about the universal phenomenon of the loss of governments's power. That is, public trust in the establishment was eroded as a result of criminal policy, as in the Vietnam War or the Watergate scandal. This reality, according to Arendt, was a "revolutionary situation" in which citizens could take the initiative, reclaim the government's lost power, and oppose it. Democracy, revolution, and civil disobedience are three names for such resistance.

The present discussion focuses on the theoretical failure of the American legal system in dealing with the phenomenon of civil disobedience to the law during the student uprising in the late 1960s, even though this form of resistance belongs to the American tradition. Unlike other countries, the founding fathers of the United States found a legitimate place for a "supreme law" on which the legal system continues to operate in some form. Its benefit is that it resolves the main legal difficulty in the relationship between federal law and the legal systems of the federation states—that "the law cannot violate the law"—by associating civil disobedience with "examining the constitutionality of this law." In reality, this doctrine was refuted when the civil rights movement's civil disobedience group became a group of opponents in the anti-Vietnam War movement who clearly broke federal law, and the Supreme Court refused to discuss the legality of the war because it was a "political question." Meanwhile, the number of people who joined the demonstrations grew, and the government's tendency to treat them as ordinary criminals or conscientious objectors who should welcome their punishment grew as well. The absurdity is that no lawyer will go to court to tell a judge that his client wants to be punished. During the turmoil of the late 1960s, insisting on such an alternative was natural. The disintegration of public service and the weakening of law enforcement capacity were the results of loss of government power. As a result, there was an increase in general crime, which created a permissive legal atmosphere (police do not have enough manpower, and prisons do not have enough space), in which the line between ordinary legal provocations and civil disobedience became increasingly blurred. Many normative citizens who took part in the protests, who had no fundamental objection to the law, were caught up in this situation.

Hence, Arendt had to be creative to theoretically defend a doctrine that a person puts the legitimacy of the law to the test by violating it. She drew inspiration for this investigation from the title of a conference held in New York in 1970: "Is the Law Dead?" Her attention was drawn to a discussion of civil-law relations in a consensual society. The central focus of her research was on analyzing citizens's relationships with the law in a "consent society," to give civil disobedience a place not only in language but also in the political system, at least in the United States. And not just based on some abstract value or a simple morality—that another morality can be imposed on top of it indefinitely. She began by defining what civil disobedience is not.

CIVIL DISOBEDIENCE VS. CONSCIENTIOUS OBJECTION

According to Arendt, in Western tradition, the character of Socrates is perceived as a paradigm of civil disobedience. It's therefore worthwhile to check what he actually said. The strange connection in the United States today between morality, consciousness, and law stems from a misconception in the case of Socrates, which ostensibly shows that disobedience to the law can be justified only if the offender wants to be punished for his action. This is why American jurists, when trying to justify civil disobedience on a moral or legal basis, always turn the case into "conscientious objection." But according to Arendt, the justification of civil disobedience is not based on consciousness or morality but political quality, that is, it stems from the publicity of the action. An individual's civil disobedience can be effective only as part of a group, an "organized minority" of citizens who are connected not through interest but a common opinion that opposes government policy even if supported by the majority of the public. Their action in concert stems from a consent between them that gives credibility and convincing proof of their opinion. In contrast, what Socrates had in common with other citizens is not an opinion but a consciousness. The problem with consciousness is that it is not generalizable, because it is possible that what I cannot live with does not bother others. Socrates's concern was not for the future of the society but only for himself—how he would live with himself—and thus his attitude was not political.

CIVIL DISOBEDIENCE VS. CRIME AND REVOLUTION

Due to the scale of the protest to which the public was exposed every day on the television screen, it had become easy to confuse civil disobedience with disobedience to the law out of criminal motives, and thus was only "reasonable" to believe President Nixon's description of the protesters as people involved in criminal behavior on the verge of treason. But as mentioned above (and will be expanded in the next section), the real reason for this attitude towards the protestors was the administration's appeal to violence due to the loss of the government's governance capability due to the loss of public trust in it. According to Arendt, criminals act in secret, while civil disobedience groups call on the public to watch how they break the law. The whole point is to get caught to show everyone that the purpose of doing so is to arouse public opinion's attention to the injustice of the government's criminal actions, in hope of restoring the legitimacy of the governing institutions they respect in the first place. Additionally, the criminal acts for his gain even if he belongs to a criminal organization. Thus he does not try to raise awareness of some injustice in the world.

And here, Arendt provides an accurate positive definition of civil disobedience. It appears when a large number of people believe that the traditional channels for change are no longer functioning and that their complaints will go unheard and unanswered—for example, during seven years of undeclared war in Vietnam, the Watergate scandal, increased Secret Service intervention in public affairs, the threat to the First Amendment's guarantee of civil liberties, an attempt to strip the Senate of its constitutional authority, the president's decision to invade Cambodia without congressional approval, constitutional accumulation of federal power at the expense of states, and so on. Civil disobedience is not a crime in any of these situations.

Finally, civil disobedience differs also from revolution for it advocates nonviolence, and, unlike revolutionaries, it accepts the framework of the establishment and the principled legitimacy of the laws.

LAW AND CHANGE

Arendt explains that the artificial political world, civilization, would not exist without stability. The legal system is one of the stabilizing factors (Roman, Greek, and Hebrew Torah). As a result, the law will be a negative force in a world that values action, as it will stifle change in times of rapid change. Only after a change has occurred can the law stabilize and make it legal, but the reason for the change is always illegal. The Supreme Court's decision on which cases to hear from those brought before it is influenced by public opinion. For instance, civil disobedience demanded that worker strikes and the right to refuse to participate in war be legalized. The United States Constitution's Fourteenth Amendment is an example of how written law cannot compel change. This section is a written translation of the changes that the Civil War brought about. However, the southern states were opposed to the change, and the racial equality provisions of the law in this section were not enforced for two hundred years. The clause was finally enforced by the Supreme Court in a decision based solely on public opinion shifts brought about by the civil rights movement's civil disobedience. Civil disobedience has brought this American dilemma to the public's attention, not the law. And this, according to Arendt, is the spirit of responsibility that the protestors inherited from the fathers of the American Revolution. As a result, in light of today's rapid changes, civil disobedience appears to be playing an important role in modern democracies. The question of its legal compliance is crucial because it will ultimately determine whether institutions entrusted with freedom will be able to withstand the onslaught of change without descending into civil war.

It was discovered, then, that the question is not whether or to what extent civil disobedience can be justified, but rather which legal concept conforms to it.

THE QUESTION OF THE OBLIGATION
TO OBEY THE LAW

The traditional answer (Rousseau, Kant) to the question of the citizen's motivation to obey the law is based on the assumption that he either agreed to it or enacted it himself. The citizen, under the rule of law, is not only subject to the will of others but also his own. That is to say, each individual is his or her own master and slave. The problem with this assumption, according to Arendt, is that the charge returns to consciousness, to the self-relationship with itself. The problem, according to modern political science, is the illusory source of consent: we are obligated to obey the majority's will. That is, we must obey the law in a democracy because we have a democratic government.

MONTESQUIEU

Arendt explains that Montesquieu observed in his 1748 book *The Spirit of Law* (*De l'Esprit des Lois*) that the spirit of law differs from state to state and between types of governments.[1] Each regime has its distinct character. The principles that operate it are its essence and the "spirit of the laws." People are motivated or inspired to operate under a particular system of laws, in one regime or another, by human desires (such as love of equality in a republic, admiration of honor in a monarchy, etc.). According to Arendt, the spirit of American law is "consent," and its uniqueness—as opposed to control—is the concept of citizens' engagement with the government. This concept, which was exercised in the colonies and later incorporated into the Union, ensures participation in all public affairs.

JOHN LOCKE

Arendt mentions three different types of social covenants that were developed in the seventeenth century. The first two are 1) biblical—people agree to accept any law that God may give them in revelation; 2) Hobbesian—everyone agrees with the secular authorities to ensure their security, and it gives them the power to do so. These two models are referred to as "vertical" by Arendt. That is, they argue for a government monopoly on power "for the subjects' physical security," implying that they are powerless themselves. Therefore, they do not fit into the American political system.

1. Arendt, *Crises of the Republic*, 68–69.

The American Republic is based on the third type, on the power of the people, similar to the Roman *potestas in populo*, in that it reserves the right to revoke the authority it has delegated to the authorities. The John Locke model, which Arendt describes as "horizontal," was the one that worked best for Americans. It is based on the principle of society's attachment (Latin: *societas*) to the government after it has established itself, limiting individual power while keeping society's power active and vital. The horizontal version has an advantage over contracts and other reciprocity-based agreements in that it is the only form of government in which independent citizens are linked together—not by historical memory or ethnic homogeneity (as in a nation-state) but by citizens' mutual promises.

According to Locke, the agreement is still valid even if the government is dissolved or if it is broken (becomes a tyranny). Even if the government collapses, society cannot return to its natural state of anarchy, once it has prepared. The power that each individual has given to society cannot be taken back, and it will always remain in the hands of the community.

In early theories of resistance, the citizen objects with his hands tied, while Locke, on the other hand, is adamant about not being chained in the first place. When the fathers of the American Revolution withdrew their lives, property, and dignity from each other when they signed the Declaration of Independence, they reflected on the revolution's experience and the conceptualization of that experience in Locke's terms.

THE DUAL NATURE OF
THE AMERICAN CONSENT SOCIETY

Every individual is born into a specific community. We all live in a state of tacit agreement when it comes to accepted norms. Because the new entrant agrees to what already exists, it's difficult to call this agreement voluntary. Only to the extent that the new entrant has a de facto legal right to object is it voluntary. The hallmark of a free government is that an individual in society knows that he is entitled to object but also knows that when he does not object, he actually agrees with the law. This is the American consent society's "dual nature." In this view, tacit consent is not a figment of the imagination, but rather a part of the human condition. As previously stated, this agreement is based on real-life experience from the prerevolutionary period, when countless contracts and alliances were formed, from the Mayflower to the unification of the thirteen colonies. According to Arendt, it's no coincidence that Locke stated: "In the beginning, the whole world was America."[2]

CONSTITUTIONAL CRISIS: WITHDRAWAL OF CONSENT

However, Arendt believes that if there is a danger of an uprising in the United States today, then it is not because of opposition to certain laws or national policies but due to the oppressive administration and extreme reluctance of parts of society to recognize the *consensus universalis*. She points out that Tocqueville predicted a hundred and fifty years ago that the great threat to the United States was not slavery, the abolition of which he anticipated, but the very continued presence of a black population in its territory. There is nothing in the Constitution or the intentions of its drafters that includes this population (or the Native Americans) in the original treaty. According to Arendt, this mistake gave rise to the tendency towards an anti-establishment attitude with an abstract morality of "condemning the whole system as an evil that allowed slavery to occur."[3] In her opinion, the current constitutional crisis stems from the degeneration of the representative system and the extreme reluctance of sections of society to recognize the "consent" in the first place and oppose reform measures.

---

2. John Locke, *Second Treatise of Civil Government* (1690), ch. 5, §49, as cited by Arendt, *Crises of the Republic*, 69.

3. Arendt, *Crises of the Republic*, 73.

THE PHENOMENON OF VOLUNTARY ASSOCIATIONS IN THE UNITED STATES

This combination of consent with the right of dissent became an organizing principle already amongst the early settlers in America, out of which the voluntary associations—which Tocqueville described with admiration in his famous book *Democracy in America* (*De la Démocratie en Amérique*) from 1835—were born. According to Arendt, his remarks are still actual: "In no country in the world has the principle of association been more successfully used, or more unsparingly applied to a multitude of different objects, than in America."[4] When the early settlers held to an idea they wished to promote or found a mistake and wanted to correct it, they always found mutual help and were no longer alone but a power that was seen and heard from the distance, whose action served as a model for all. According to Arendt, the massive demonstrations against the war organized by the student movement in Washington prove the actuality of this tradition in America today. In fact, civil disobedience is the latest form of those ancient voluntary associations.

Arendt continues to rely on Tocqueville also in his warnings that a joint march in which no one is committed to a single path can be as horrible as in Europe where the march was controlled by a repulsive force whose support was even less than in the government it is opposing. Indeed, I can attest that during my frequent support visits to the permanent protest encampment in front of the prime minister's residence in Balfour, I became acquainted with the existence of power circles within that camp and was sometimes warned not to talk to Netanyahu supporters and "Kahanists"[5] who

4. Tocqueville, *Democracy in America*, 213.

5. Followers of the far-right political leader, Rabbi Meir Kahane, who was finally barred from election to the Israeli parliament in the late eighties. Strangely, Kahane's case fits into the framework of my discussion of American and Israeli politics. Some have recently traced the influence of the New Left's resistance and blacks' violent struggle against the American liberal establishment and its egalitarian values in the 1960s on the young Kahane, who saw these values as a threat to Jewish identity. Out of distrust in the establishment's

used to pass by the place to confront the protesters. That is, voluntary associations can be tyrannical. However, Tocqueville thought that the risk was worthy, because through these voluntary associations the Americans were learning the art of reducing the danger of tyranny; because when we are within such associations, we must meet people with whom we do not agree, and through this experience, we learn what it means to be a free democratic citizen.

And, finally, the real threat to the student movement—which was the main civil disobedience group in Arendt's time—was a clinging to ideologies.

Arendt concludes that in reality, even though civil disobedience complements the American law, the only lawbreaker known to the court is the *conscientious objector*, and the only group organization they know is "conspiracy." Therefore civil disobedience is the only modern way to return citizens to self-government and thus should be constitutionally legitimized. Although civil disobedience is already a worldwide phenomenon, it is substantially still a novelty of Americans. For example, it has no word in any other language. That is why the American Republic is the only government that can deal with it, through what Arendt calls the "spirit of the laws." The U.S. owes its existence to the American Revolution, which brought with it a new idea—though not completely defined—of law, which was not the result of a theory but was created from the special experience of the early colonies before the

_____

ability to overcome the racism embedded in white society, he encouraged his followers to use force to defend their identity, as blacks did. He also supported the war in Vietnam. And later, he attempted to implement this strategy in Israel, which he saw as a conduit for Jewish aggression as well as the ultimate bastion against equality and democracy. To that end, he equated the black struggle in America with the liberal *Ashkenazi* establishment's alleged repression of *Mizrachis*. His militant racist messages remain popular among *Shas*, a religiously ethnic-Oriental party, and the *national religious* sector. These overlapping camps have given rise to a younger generation that sees liberalism, the left, and Ashkenazim as a unified foe. Itamar Ben Gvir, one such *Mizrachi* Kahanist, is now a rising public figure. After joining the *Likud* with Netanyahu's support, he appears to have turned it into a populist Kahanist gang that abandoned the elitist secular agenda that traditionally characterized it. Furthermore, Ben Gvir was recently viewed as a replacement leader for Netanyahu.

revolution. According to Arendt, finding it a constitutional niche will be a historic event that equals the event of the founding of the Constitution itself. Therefore, the first step would introduce civil disobedience into our political language, such as recognizing civil disobedience minorities as other minorities, so they will become not only a force seen from afar in demonstrations but always present, a factor taken into account. However, since state institutions in the representative regime are a failure and the regime's authority has lost its vitality, the real urgency in the U.S. today is to introduce something to the political system through anchoring in the constitution, i.e., to change the definition of voluntary associations to "civil disobedience groups," and the right to "dissent" to "resistance."

DISCUSSION

Initially, one would wonder whether a political protest must be linked to a legal infringement. According to Arendt, the constitutional crisis that was expressed in the government's illegal activities during the Vietnam War, as well as the fact that courts functioned according to the dictates of political doctrine, proves that the establishment did not totally vanish but simply lost the people's faith. The historical experience of Germany, America, and, more recently, Israel demonstrates that the tendency—particularly among intellectuals—to trust that the courts "will always be there for us" is catastrophic. Civic activism is more credible. However, the so-called Movement for Quality of Government in Israel is vital to the country's survival, so it must be nurtured. Arendt claims, therefore, that we have sources of resistance other than the courts, such as civil disobedience and voluntary organizations.

Where can we find such a genuine American spirit today? In my opinion, Arendt would have welcomed new voluntary political forms from the left and right, such as Black Lives Matter or the Tea Party in America, as well as organizations like Black Flags, Crime Minister, and the Movement for Quality of Government in Israel, as the latest version of the movement for civil rights. They all acted in a way that is characteristic of genuine politics. One should rejoice in the fact that people are engaged in public affairs, that they dissent. When they see injustice or anything wrong, they band together on the streets, not only demonstrating but even breaking the law to get their message through in a way that matters to others. As a result, the American concept of citizens' right to dissent in circumstances where their government is deteriorating is also being implemented in Israel.

Some people in Israel are concerned that the left no longer has a central narrative. However, according to Arendt's political theory, politics isn't expected to have any content other than political activity itself, which is the meeting of free people in a free public realm to argue nonviolently in speech how to share a shared world. Arendt, in my opinion, would have been interested in seeing how these volunteer groupings of demonstrators against Netanyahu's criminal administration come together to establish a counter-politics she would name *natality*, a fresh example of a political form that can emerge in the face of bad politics. She would have been astounded by the scope of the project. This protest movement was one of the most significant in the country's history. To sum, there is no "left" in the Marxist sense, no "narrative," only "resistance." In fact, the right wing stuck the "left" label on the protestors.

Arendt observed that the amnesia of the revolutionary spirit of the United States' founding fathers—who composed the Constitution—is scary, since normative citizens "behave astonishingly illegally" in the eyes of the state, to the point where, if the police were to ban a large number of people, the courts and jails would be overwhelmed. When compared to the Israeli protests, the initial arrest of Mr. Amir Haskel, a key figure in the movement and a senior retired Air Force officer, raised an eyebrow even among some on the right. The ridiculous cause for this arrest—straying from the sidewalk—was, of course, confirmation that the phenomena of civil disobedience in front of Prime Minister Netanyahu's home had entered a legal gray area. The establishment appeared to be making every effort to incriminate the protestors. The prime minister, his son, and his faithful cabinet ministers dubbed them "anarchists," "corona deniers," or "traitors," echoing President Nixon's description of anti-war protestors in Washington as persons engaged in risky activities on the verge of treason. There is no such thing as a constitution in Israel, and there is no such thing as a "spirit of the law" in whose name an interpretation may be sought in support of citizens acting in concert in the public domain in front of the prime minister's residence. Yet there is something akin to what Robert Dahl refers to as an "unwritten constitution"[6] in Israel, namely an attitude of mutual responsibility that arose from the collectivity that defined the country in its early years, particularly in the army, and subsequently spread to other aspects of life. However, such an ethos, in my opinion, can no longer exist in the reality of a mass society devoid of common public ambitions, where the public arena is dominated by commercial considerations manipulated by an unholy covenant between corporations and governments.

6. Dahl, *How Democratic*, 159–60.

CHAPTER 4

The Phenomenon of the Praise
of Violence in the 1960s

THE ESSAY "ON VIOLENCE" touches on many of the issues raised
in the previous texts, including the false prestige of experts in
government service, the collapse of civil service, the decline of
public trust in the establishment, the fall of the American revolutionary tradition into oblivion, and another aspect of the African
American issue in her discussion about race—because of which
it is a criticized article. These observations on the matter of race
are important to my examination of the Israeli setting that fol-
lows the current discussion, along with the degeneration of the
representative system, the "ideological sin" of student revolt, that
is, a consideration of the negative aspects of the student uprising,
which was right in itself. However, what made this text popular
and massively quoted was its discussion on power and violence,
which was innovative at the time.

Arendt's observations here are in response to events and debates in the twentieth century, which, as Lenin predicted, became
a century of wars and revolutions, and therefore a century with
violence as its lowest common denominator. Given the importance of violence in human affairs, she believes it is odd that it
has never been addressed per se. Renan, for example, believed it
was overlooked since it was unintentional, erroneous, and so not

"serious."[1] Violence, according to Clausewitz, is "the continuation of politics by other means"[2]—that is, it is minor and insignificant. It has even yet to be included in an encyclopedia.

VIOLENCE AND ITS INSTRUMENTS

The first section of the article discusses the phenomenon of violence in Western culture, as well as Arendt's claim that foreign policy—which has become purely violent due to the fatal nature of weapons of mass destruction in the nuclear age (total war)—is a problem with no solution, at least as long as nation-states exist. In this regard, the United States is unique because the term "sovereignty" did not appear in the Constitution. But the times of proud detachment from the continental conceptual and linguistic, traditional framework of the nation-state have passed. The legacy of the eighteenth-century American Revolution was forgotten, and the American government—for better or worse—reentered the European tradition without paying heed to Europe's collapse in strength, the bankruptcy of the nation-state, and the idea of their sovereignty.

The Boomerang Effect and the Cultural Climate behind the New Left's Pathos

As the instruments of violence became dubious and uncertain in international relations, they gained a reputation in domestic affairs. That is, everything today is foreign policy. The boomerang effect is reflected in the escalating violence among young revolutionaries and on the part of police brutality. Hence Arendt assumes that

1. "Those who saw nothing but violence in human affairs, convinced that they were 'always haphazard, not serious, not precise' (Renan) or that God was forever with the bigger battalions, had nothing more to say about either violence or history" (Arendt, *Crises of the Republic*, 87). Arendt is most likely referring to Ernest Renan's "Qu'est-ce qu-une nation?" from a presentation at the Sorbonne on March 11, 1882; see Renan, *What Is a Nation?*, pt. 1.

2. Clausewitz, *On War*, 87.

student violence is linked to this bizarre suicidal development of modern weapons. The attraction to weapons not only for defense purposes stems from a pathos that combines fear with admiration for the success of violence. This is a generation that heard the tick-tock of the bomb. At the same time, they saw foreign policy's violence as a successful model for accomplishing political and social goals, and they incorporated it into the distorted Marxist ideology they adhered to. Arendt also mentions the young people's environment, which was characterized by a culture that glorified violence. She examines certain irresponsible remarks made by neo-Marxists such as Frantz Fanon, George Sorrell, and Jean-Paul Sartre, who attributed to the Marxist revolution violence that Marx did not say and did not mean, which affected the students's erroneous perspective of Marx. In his 1908 essay *Reflections on Violence (Reflexions sur la violence)*, Sorrell sought to develop a fusion of Marxism with a Bergsonian philosophy of life. Through this merger, he understood the class struggle in military terms, and concluded that there is nothing more violent than a "general strike,"[3] which at the time earned him the title Fascist. Fanon, a black post-colonialist from the National Front for the Liberation of Algeria, claimed in his book *The Wretched of the Earth* (1961), which deals with the benefits of violence, that it is better to be hungry than to be a slave and eat bread. Sartre, who combined Marxism and existentialism and spoke of violent protest, wrote in the preface to Fanon's book in a paraphrase of his last words that only what caused harm can heal it.[4] According to Arendt, the impact of the late Sartre war experience led him to the idea of violent necessity; although the students did not experience a war like him, they resorted to violence under his influence. Sartre is, therefore, an example of how the students were unaware of the distance between their favorite Marxist thinkers and Marx himself. However, Arendt goes on to say that, despite the left's apparent adoration of violence, historically, the right wing has been more deadly. Reading the students' nonsense

3. Sorrell, *Reflections on Violence*, ch. 4 ("The Proletarian Strike").

4. "For violence, like Achilles' lance, can heal the wounds it has inflicted" (Sartre, "Preface," 30).

yields an image of reintroduction of a salad of ideas that Marx had previously dismissed as irrelevant to the revolution, including the "third world" illusion (inspired by the call of Sartre and Herbert Marcuse). Apart from the fact that this is another deviation from Marx—who thought that the reality of slave revolt was a slandered thing—the more serious problem is that the term "third world" does not express reality but ideology. In any case, this too was part of the pathos of the "new left."

Parallel to their "ideology sin," namely adherence to old theories that were themselves confusing, they acted politically positive in three ways: belief in their ability to change things, having a moral argument, and demanding to participate in university administration. Arendt managed to hear one genuine slogan for medicine among their plethora of vanity slogans: their demand for "participatory democracy," because it is derived from the best of the revolutionary tradition—the "council system," egalitarian and spontaneous, small, voluntary, popular associations that sprang up across the country during modern revolutions, a method destroyed anytime and anywhere, whether directly by nation-state bureaucracies or by the party machines.

Their protest against the academy's backing for military purposes was equally valid, implying that the riots around the scientific crisis and the crisis of faith in "progress" are not caused by intergenerational conflict, but rather by the fact that nuclear science is a brand-new thing. The academy is meant to be a place free of the influence of society and those in positions of power. However, this protest was combined with a demand that the academy be returned to the people, which was manifested, among other things, in the occupation of administrative buildings on campuses (e.g., at Columbia University). In the first place, the American student protest was nonviolent in principle. According to Arendt, one can perceive in these invasions where they held huge sit-ins the use of property that to some extent belongs also to them. The police's harsh response was the catalyst for their extremism. This, according to Arendt, is a good aspect of protest: this generation is characterized psychologically by pure courage, a startling urge for action, and a surprising trust in the possibility of change.

On the other hand, Arendt was opposed to an armed rebellion, especially with the emergence of the Black Power movement on campuses, which meant that African-Americans brought actual violence into the student uprising rather than just rhetoric, as well as some whites' demand that the universities be closed due to their corruption. According to Arendt, all of this will destroy universities and cut off the branch on which the student movement rests. According to her, the desire for equal rights has led to the admission of many African-Americans without basic skills, and subservience to their demand—due to the shock of integration that gripped them—for their own curriculum (African studies, for example) lowered white standards to their level. According to Arendt, this is an easy way to get rid of their problems. She cites the idea that what these kids need is some redeeming practice, which includes studying math and understanding how to correctly write one phrase in English.

All this has to do with keeping the cause of the uprising away from public support outside the university. Black violence, according to Arendt, was similar to working-class violence a decade before, when there was a broad social consensus. And it is here that the new left, despite its remarkable loyalty to the past, embodied in the moral nature of the Marxist rebellion, clashes with Marx once more. All of modern history's revolutionary movements were led by people who did not consider themselves revolutionaries but were motivated by compassion or a desire for justice. From the beginning, Marxist revolutionaries have accepted and connected with the workers' practical, nonspeculative concerns. As a result, they were provided with a solid base within society. And that, the young white rebels could not achieve despite their efforts to find allies, unlike African-American students who were rooted in established neighborhoods and black social movements, and thus in a better position for negotiating with the establishment. According to Arendt, the university's concession to the demands of the African American student movement to lower the admissions standard and allow individuals without training derives from white guilt. This shows that the academy is willing to accept such a protest coupled with violence, implying that violence is a successful social persuasive tool, but not in the case of the white student demonstration, which was nonviolent.

Violence and the Modern Idea of Progress

Regarding criticism against the content of the curriculum, the students expressed resentment from what they saw as celebration of science. Arendt explains that Marx took from Hegel the metaphor of the dialectic, according to which every society has a seed of the next society, and this is the only certainty of the movement of progress in history. However, whereas Hegel turns to the past to understand how we came to the present, Marx looks from the present point forward to the future to provide an answer to the troubling question "Where do we go from here?" That is, the concept of introduction became a guideline for future action: let's do something better! According to Arendt, this idea is an illusion today. This is just a metaphor, that is, the forefront of the entire human race guarantees nothing to the individual except his death, which we already know. The idea of progress exists to this day thanks to the remarkable achievements of natural science in the nineteenth century that revealed the secrets of the universe, which indeed are in infinite progress. The classic notion of progress does not correspond to scientific progress today and thus cannot be used to measure processes in the realm of human affairs. The young students argued that the growing demand in universities for natural science scholars has led to pseudo-scholarship, knowing more and more about less and less. Arendt adds that today's progress is no longer about how we become rational or about our character (Marx's new human vision) but is seen as economic progress, the accumulation of property, the hunger for "ownership of more," which characterizes political and economic theories. For example, the answer of the liberal economic conception today to Marx's question "Where do we go from here?" is: let us start something bigger, better. But nothing unexpected came out of it, only "necessary" results of what we already knew. This is in contrast to our historical experience, which shows a lot of unexpected things—including the student revolt itself. According to Arendt, the natural sciences not only transcended the earth but also transcended the economic realm. Man is subject to manipulation due to his greed. Violence is used as a tool for manipulation (shaping thoughts by the media, disinformation), and therefore scholarship that has ceased to be real is related to the increase in violence.

Arendt concludes that if we continue to view history as a continuous chronological process whose progression is necessary, then the only thing that may disrupt such automatic processes is violence in the shape of war or revolution. And if that's the case, then today's student uprising's new preachers of violence were correct. In other words, violence can be used as a substitute for action in some instances. And this is one of the article's primary points: violence is justifiable only when it is used in the name of revolution and only under specific circumstances.

POWER AND ITS RELATION TO VIOLENCE

Arendt begins the second part of the article with a review of selected views in the field of political theory (Max Weber, Charles W. Mills, Bertrand de Jouvenel, Robert Strausz-Hupé, Alexander P. d'Entreves), only to discover, to her surprise, that both the right and left agree that violence is the blatant use of force and that effective power is ultimately the muzzle of the gun. According to Mills, politics is all about power battles, which culminate in bloodshed. And, according to Jouvenel, leadership is possible only because of impulse control. Subordinating others to one's will makes one feel more human and gives one more joy. That is, there is no such thing as power without a command and an attitude of obedience—a position similar to Sartre's. Even d'Entreves, the only one who was aware of the important difference between force and violence, did not get to the root of the matter by defining force as moderate violence or institutional force. That is, it is no different from the others mentioned here. According to Arendt, these positions were derived from the concept of absolute power that accompanied the emergence of the sovereign nation-state, whose speakers were Jean Bodin in sixteenth-century France and Thomas Hobbes in seventeenth-century England. And they also correspond to the Platonic tradition of forms of human rule over man that have passed down in history since ancient Greece. As I previously stated, there was another political tradition for her, namely the Homeric experience, which understood power as having something to do with community activity: self-government (*isonomia*), i.e., participatory democracy, which the Romans revived to some extent in their own version (*civitas*). In these two types of governance, they sought a law that was not the same as force of rule. According to Arendt, this is the paradigm that eighteenth-century revolutionaries in America discovered in archives that inspired them to construct a republic based on people's power rather than human control over man, which belongs to a slave society.

Against this background, Arendt provides a linguistic explication of the terms of power, force, violence, authority, and so on, in order to finally dispel that embarrassing confusion. Arendt is not an analytical philosopher, but she has a habit of exacerbating the discrepancies between concepts in all of her writings. She claims that if we want to have a real discussion about anything at all, we must do so. There is a proclivity to generate new meanings that blur the distinctions between terminologies.

In politics, for example, the issue has always been, "Who controls whom?" Only when we stop reducing human affairs to "control" will the actual data, with all of its differences and authentic diversity, be rediscovered:

a. Power refers to a person's ability to act in concert with others. Power does not belong to an individual, but rather to a group, and it remains with the group as long as the group is together. When we say that someone "has the power," we mean that he has received the power of a certain number of people. When the group disbands, that man's power dissipates as well. The word power is already a metaphor when used nowadays to describe someone with power or a strong personality. We mean force without the metaphor.

b. Strength is a quality that is ingrained in a person's character and manifests itself in their interactions with others but is not dependent on them. Many people have a natural desire to destroy it, since it is special and autonomous.

c. Force is the release of physical or social energy, such as that of natural forces or the necessity of circumstances. It is associated with violence in daily English, especially when employed for coercion.

d. Authority is the most elusive of all concepts, making it vulnerable to abuse. Its distinguishing feature is that individuals who are required to obey it recognize it. It does not require any coercion or persuasion. As a result, a parent who hits his son—or, on the other hand, treats him equally—loses his authority. The validity of authority is a mark of respect for the person who wields it or for his position. Contempt is authority's worst foe, and the most effective way to challenge it is to ridicule it.

e. Violence. Its instrumentality distinguishes it. It is phenomenologically similar to strength. The power of violent tools, like any other tool, is created to replicate natural strength until, at the end of development, the tools replace it.

Why Do We Confuse Them?

According to Arendt, in fact, violence and power often appear to be combined together. It's uncommon to come across them in their purest form. And the inclination to associate power with violence when discussing governance derives from the temptation (because of prejudice) to think of authority in terms of imperative and obedience.

Arendt's main point is that power and violence are opposites—where one rules, the other is absent. True political power derives its legitimacy from numbers (amount of opinions) rather than instruments (few armed men can control masses of people). Violence is justified only when used for a short term—for example, in order to stop automatic processes—otherwise, it will lead to more violence and consequently to a nonpolitical world. And only justified when it is by the hands of revolutionaries, and not by governments (which turn it into a policy of terror).

Terrorism is a type of government that emerges after violence has obliterated all power—and remains in full control. To initiate a full-scale terror campaign, all resistance must be removed. A network of informers is used to accomplish this.

In line with the core premise of her political theory and under the influence of the founding fathers of the American Revolution, Arendt says that all forms of government are based on plurality or the viewpoints of diverse people. After all, even a tyrant needs the loyalty of his secret police. As a result, in terms of the propensity for violence among rebellious students, when the power of any sort of government is lost, there is no longer a necessity for violent action against a smashed system.

But even an impotent government (one that has lost its power, i.e., public support) will persist as long as there are no rebels willing to grab the power spread in the streets and assume responsibility for it. That is, when a force disintegrates, a revolution can occur, resulting in what Arendt refers to as a "revolutionary state of things."[5] However, the revolution is no longer required. And this is exactly what happened in France during the student uprising. To the astonishment of the young rebels, who had intended only to challenge the university system, the entire political system, including all of its bureaucracy, crumbled in front of their eyes, and even President de Gaulle escaped to Germany. However, none of the student leaders accepted responsibility for the power that they wielded on the streets. Ironically, the president was the one who reclaimed power from the military, i.e., via consent rather than obedience.

5. Arendt, *Crises of the Republic*, 118.

FURTHER CLARIFICATION OF THE REASONS FOR THE VIOLENCE

According to Arendt, vast sums of money have been expended in numerous studies of violence and aggression in the social and natural sciences. There has been a flood of books published on the subject, and even a new science has been developed. Despite this, she has something to add to the topic. She opens the article's last section with a critique of what she sees as futile attempts by the scientific and social sciences to understand the causes of violence. According to the biologist Portman, what we know about ourselves occurs in animals as well. That is all there is to it. But in Arendt's opinion, with this approach, we return to the reality that the human behavior index is based on animal behavior.

She, on the other hand, claims that violence is neither monstrous nor unreasonable, since it is employed to achieve a goal, to express a message, and thus it is a part of human emotional life. In terms of the link between violence and rage, Arendt claims that the solution of violence in absurd instances is more appealing due to the immediacy of violence. However, the quickness with which violence reacts does not make it illogical. On the contrary, it is precisely this rapidity that provides redemption in both private and public issues. In some cases, the only option to restore justice is to act without debate or to speak without respect for consensus. In this regard, aggression and rage are also natural human emotions, and thus the endeavor to heal a person of violence and rage is to castrate or dehumanize him. When it comes to the connection between violence and hypocrisy, Arendt emphasizes that words are believable only if you can be sure they expose rather than conceal. When reasoning is used as a trap, it makes no sense to utilize logic. It is not irrational to use a gun for self-defense. However, in the event of the student uprising, justified violence against hypocrisy, according to Arendt, loses its right to exist. That is, when it is rationalized (with strategy and aims, i.e., ideology), it becomes irrational, as Robespierre discovered once the psychological hunt for underlying motives began.

In response to Fanon's claim that violence is a sign of life that produces a new person who establishes a state based on friendships and Sorrell's claim that working-class people are willing to create a new moral quality needed to improve production, namely a fighting spirit without hatred or revenge or seeking honor and glory, values absent from the bourgeoisie, Arendt wonders why we should not conclude that an act of violence is a special right of young people, i.e., those who are supposed to be full of life? Indeed, the younger generation's revolutionary mentality today is characterized by a common mix of violence, vitality, and creativity. For them, the joys of life and the joys of violence are one and the same, i.e., the emphasis on the facts of life, such as making love, for hippies, is a reaction to the machine's doomsday, which will wipe out all life on earth. Yet, the new left's categories are not new. According to Arendt, social productivity as a reflection of life dates back to Marx. Belief in violence as a force that supports life dates back to Nietzsche, and belief in creativity as the most sublime human trait dates back to Bergson.

Finally, there is no bigger threat than organic thinking infiltrating politics, which interprets power and violence in biological terms. The metaphors used in the discourse on riots, such as "sick society" and the like, are similar to medical experts' discourse on surgery. As the use of biological analogies becomes more prevalent, the likelihood that individuals will act as if they were in the animal world increases. Violence and power are not natural phenomena, i.e., expressions of life processes, but rather part of the political dimension of human affairs, which is essentially guaranteed by the human capacity for action, i.e., the ability to begin something new.

Special Modern Causes

Arendt maintained in the first part of the article that the students' violence was caused by a combination of fear and admiration for weapons. She now extends this argument to other fears stemming from borderlessness, such as government size, displeasure with the bureaucratization of public life, and the administration's repression, which intellectuals essentially control. This is the book *Crises of the Republic*'s ultimate argument—again, contrary to popular belief—that violence in modernity stems from the fact that even liberal-democratic welfare states have "solved" the problem of their inability to rule ever-increasing populations through oppressive and bombastic administration. The "rule of nobody" is the bureaucratization of public life and the scorn for bureaucracy, civil service, and the intellectuals ("experts") who run the show.

The Size Problem

Part of the advancement of the modern age has been determined through an attitude of more and more, bigger and bigger. And as the country grows in terms of population, objects, and assets, so will the need for administration and with it the anonymous power of the administrators to control the mass society. The process of transforming the government into an administration or a republic into a bureaucracy, as well as the retreat of the public sphere that has accompanied it, has intensified in the last century, owing to the emergence of the representational system's party bureaucracy. Action, more than any other human ability, has suffered the most as a result of all of this. If acting and starting are the same thing, the inflated system of the parties has succeeded in suppressing all citizens' actions, even in countries where freedom of speech is guaranteed.

Arendt's point is that in this "rule of nobody," there is a feeling that nothing can be changed, the responsibility is passed down from clerk to clerk. Bureaucracy makes people feel powerless. And if everyone is helpless, there is tyranny without tyranny, the most severe form of tyranny because no one knows who to complain to. And there is no "enemy" when it comes to a yearning for revolution. According to Arendt's political theory, bureaucracy is a "despair of action" or a "suspension of action" (in German: *Praxisentzug*), that creates a deep antagonism toward the establishment, that people identify it with the intellectuals who run it, with no less rage than the French people had against the aristocrats during the French Revolution, or rebels against King George during the American Revolution. Bureaucracies encourage violence by obliterating bonds with the people they control. Arendt mentions in this context the claim of the Czech writer Pavel Kohout, who supported the attempts to reform and democratize communism in his country during the "Prague Spring" of 1968, according to which, if there is no new proper example of defining a free citizen as a "participant-citizen," humanity will sink in the next millennium into an era of "highly civilized monkeys" or alternatively become a society of rats, ruled by an elite that draws its power from the "smart advice" of intellectuals. They will believe that computers can think instead of people. According to Arendt, Kohout was aiming for "participatory democracy."

New Nationalism: Opposition to Centralism

Arendt points to the emergence of a new type of right-wing nationalism that is related to opposition to "bigness" per se. Unlike in the past, when national feelings tended to unite diverse ethnic groups across the country through political sentiments, we now observe how ethnic nationalism threatens to destabilize nation-states. In their struggle against centralist administrations, ethnic groups such as the Scots, Welsh, and Basques in Spain are demanding separation. Surprisingly, despite the failure of size impact, the United States has just embarked on a fresh attempt at a centralist administration that gives the federal government far greater power than the states. However, it appears that this most prosperous European colony wishes to share the destiny of the mother countries (continental nation-states) when they reach the end of their days. That is, it hurriedly repeats the same errors that the Constitution's drafters attempted to correct and eliminate. Administrativization and centralization always have the same political outcome: monopolization of power causes all legitimate sources of power in a country to dry up. We face not only the breakdown of the power structure but also the power itself, which is still active and ineffective in the United States, which is founded on the plurality of forces, their oversight, and mutual balancing. We are confronted with power's impotence. The power of students is trampled by party bureaucracy, just as Congress's power was stomped, trampled by the president.

While it is impossible to predict where all of this will lead, Arendt concludes that every drop of power is an invitation to violence. There is no empty void. She isn't as terrified of revolutionaries but more of governments: those in power who believe it has slipped from their grasp will succumb to the temptation to replace it with violence, which can easily devolve into terror. In her opinion, the riots in black ghettos and the revolts on college campuses make people feel as if they are acting in concert in a rare way. Even if it isn't just a manifestation of an ultimate loss of human action, it is neither an activity that leads to the new example that Pavel Kohut had hoped for. Given the collapse of powers under their size, this "new example" appears to have a chance only in small countries or small sectors that are well defined as islands inside the mass societies of the big powers.

Summary of Arendt's Main Arguments

The main argument in the middle part of the article is against the dominant conception of power in political thought, according to which violence is an expression of extreme power. We must therefore be vigilant and ensure that the public sphere remains free for action. There is no vacuum—where manifestations of genuine political action are absent, tools for distorted expressions of the ability to act, that is, false forms of politics, appear. The deception could be motivated by a desire for change; ideology provides a "safe haven" for meaninglessness; violence is a tempting substitute for power; and from the distinction between power and violence, the connection to the article on civil disobedience becomes clear. The more violence there is, the less power there is—power is found to be a form of resistance, and civil disobedience is a form of power.

Another argument (in the first and last parts) is that violence is legitimate in a particular context of revolutions, but not when it is in the hands of governments. Of all the forms of false politics, Arendt finds not only in lying but also in violence something genuine. She has sympathy for the violence of social movements because popular violence sometimes has genuine goals and is a substitute for action in case there is nothing else capable of interfering in an automatic process. This is in contrast to the official violence of the state, which is intended to cause support for its institutions and not agreement between citizens. In the twentieth century, the means of violence became so destructive that it could no longer be justified. So what is the limit of violence on the part of revolutionaries? The short-term goal and the use of spot violence is to promote change. If the French students had not "turned tables," there would have been no reform of education in France to this day.

The third argument (which appears in the last part of the article) is that violence is not monstrous (animalistic) but completely rational, because it needs a goal that will justify it. But as stated, it must be a short-term goal.

From this, Arendt strengthens the previous argument for justifying the violence.

Violence can be just, it has a hidden rationale, it expresses a human need (belongs to legitimate human feelings)—and even though society condemns it, it has a place in politics. But violence is limited because it is not a substitute for authority, it does not build power. In the long run, if the change that revolutionaries wish for fails, violence will remain. The world will become more violent and not more political.

Arendt actually reaches the bottom line of *Crises of the Republic* in the last discussion of the article: a complete revolution, not just reform, is required because the oppression of the administration and the bureaucratization of public life destroy the relationship between government and citizens. According to her, the students' reaction to this scenario altered the protest's focus from a revolution against oppressors to a moral debate over government form. The question is, what causes opposition to become a true revolution? And how can a revolution overcome all of the issues raised by Arendt? This will be at the heart of the discussion about the student rebellion in the next chapter where she will elaborate on concepts like "revolutionary situation," "real analysis of the existing situation," and "council system" that she mentioned in passing here.

Discussion

Arendt's critique of the "sin of ideology" of students in America and Germany is that effective protest movement requires a language that reflects the political moment of the general public in the present, rather than a repetition of ideas from the past. This is in line with one of the key insights in her book *On Revolution*, that although the revolution's fathers were educated people, the revolution itself was carried out by people with no theoretical background. In this regard, protest groups and activists in Israel followed moral values rather than ideologies. They didn't engage with left or right, or theories, for that matter. Although red flags of various socialist movements were occasionally seen during the demonstrations, they were a minority, and no one seemed to take their message seriously. The majority of the activists concentrated on the issue at hand, notably the Netanyahu government's corruption, and attempted to persuade others to join them.

According to Arendt, even leftists who struggle for democracy mistake "power" and "force," because violence usually referred to as "power" is itself a sort of false politics prevalent today. In this regard, the anti-Netanyahu protest movement was primarily made up of ad hoc volunteer organizations that demanded the strengthening of democracy and occasionally engaged in civil disobedience—that is, they were two legitimate resistance forces against control and violence. As a result, Arendt's distinction that political assassination was historically, aside from a few deeds of small fringe anarchist groups, a particular prerogative reserved for the right, aligns precisely with the depiction of the forces at work during the events in Israel.

The inciting of top right-wing politicians by Netanyahu—which was quickly translated into physical terror of their supporters on the streets—was intended to destroy the genuine political power accumulated by protestors. The disproportionate use of violent instruments by the police, as well as the aggression of Netanyahu's fans (particularly the criminal promiscuous component, such as La Familia gang), are examples of what might happen when governments have control over violence. As a result, I think that Netanyahu's statements that the violent behavior of his followers is justified by the aggression of those protesting against him cannot be accepted in light of Arendt's concept of power and violence.

Regarding what Arendt views as a phenomenon of rebellion against a mysterious intellectual elite that allegedly runs the establishment, the so-called oriental (in Hebrew: *Mizrachi*, i.e., Jewish-Israelis of North African and Asian descent) right-wing supporters located on the periphery, who have traditionally been seen as a classic oppressed working-class sector and traditionally a support base for right-wing governments since the 1977 coup, conform (in view of Herbert Marcuse's thesis) to the current political order. It appears that they prefer the economic and technological benefits that capitalism—which was heavily promoted under Netanyahu's rule—brings. The so-called left is the only group that opposes the neutralization of political action caused by the unholy alliance between capital and government, which has resulted in the domestication of consumer culture in the (supposed to be free) public sphere, the collapse of civil service (welfare, education), and the loss of trust in political parties. So much so, that many old school lefties today sound like what was considered "extreme left" four decades ago. Nevertheless, the protests were carried out using a civil disobedience strategy, which is another response to felt powerlessness and alienattion. "Let us fight for our right to be heard, let us resist!" says civil disobedience. But, just as American students' efforts to persuade the working class to join their struggle for a more egalitarian and just society in the late 1960s were fruitless, any attempt by anti-Netanyahu protesters to engage Netanyahu's supporters in even a basic conversation about issues like economic and social justice was a deaf discourse.

The problem of intellectual elite hostility connects to the preceding chapter's consideration of the consent crisis. Even if there were few opponents of the bureaucratization of public life among the peripheral Mizrachi right wingers during the protest, they were swallowed up by an anti-establishment attitude motivated by an abstract morality of condemning the entire establishment as evil, because it allowed the sin against oriental Jewish newcomers during the fifties to occur. The paradox is that numerous right-wingers—including a sizable number of Mizrachi Israelis—are the ones who fill key posts in the Israeli government monster. The popular oriental right-wingers' rhetoric, as well as that of the intellectuals who supported them (with all sorts of pseudo-theses on a "continuation of the rule of the old Ashkenazi elites") continually deflected the public debate on the legitimacy of Netanyahu's policy, to the level of some emotive cosmic ethnic battle. Right-wing Mizrachi youths made statements about Yitzhak Rabin as a traitor, David Ben Gurion as a colonialist trafficking Mizrachi Jewish slaves, or Kibbutzniks (Israeli expression for people who grew up in Kibbutz) as "state's land robbers"—revealing that significant sections of Israeli society do not see themselves, and never have, as part of an all-encompassing national consensus. As previously discussed in the section on political lying, history can be read in a variety of ways, but not in the sense that Ben Gurion invaded England. In view of Arendt's distinction regarding the extremism of African-American organizations in the United States, the Israeli Mizrachi right wing enjoys speculating that some parts of the Israeli public do not agree with the idea of civic equality and do not accept their presence. As a result, they criticize the entire establishment as wicked. Thus, they treated the protest against Netanyahu as a symbol of the ancient Ashkenazi logos, relics of heirs of the primordial elite sin. The abstract morality of this anti-establishment attitude also explains the right-wing Mizrachi public's historical refusal to try integration (as well as the rejection of former Prime Minister

Ehud Barak's reconciliation attempts), as if they preferred some Israeli version of "Colonia in Liberia," or some kind of what Arendt
calls "new nationalism." Similar to the case of African Americans,
this approach delayed reform. The Mizrachi right is anti-political
because it has instilled violence into a public space where politics
is supposed to be conducted through speech and persuasion, and
therefore their leaders do not adhere to nonviolent practices in
civil disobedience, similar to African American leaders in the late
1960s. From the point of view of the idea of the "consent society,"
the protest of change divided the people of Israel into two camps:
Only Netanyahu vs. Only Not Netanyahu.

The question now is whether there is a deeper explanation
for the Mizrachi right wing's opposition? On the right and the left,
there is currently a phenomenon of international opposition to
the existing order. And there are opportunists who use this dis-
agreement to bolster fascist organizations by stating that they are
"defending the nation-state" against immigrants and foreigners.
Arendt refers to this as the "new nationalism." And these fascist
minds are erecting a bureaucracy that is unconcerned about the
welfare of the country. It's just a means of gaining power.

The dilemma we confront today is the emergence of the populist right, which was at its peak in the United States until recently
and is still dominating in countries like Hungary, Venezuela, Turkey, and Israel.

In one of her earlier essays, Arendt argued that the Nazis
transformed nihilism, which had existed for sixty to one hundred
years, from a sublime philosophical idea about the loss of values
(relativism, which means that there are many truths but nothing
we truly believe in) into a practical expression of poisoned intoxi-
cation for destruction in the 1930s. Nazism arose from the void
left by the breakdown of Germany's social and political structures.
They addressed a community of disgruntled citizens who had lost
faith in the country as a result of military defeat and rising in-
flation, and told them chauvinistic militant slogans that they are
exceptional (*Volksgemeinschaft*)—which excludes other peoples.
There's no better feeling than going to kill them. The tremendous

psychological attraction of the Nazis (apart from false promises) was related to the sincere identification of the void. Their success stemmed from the fact that they were fully aware of its power, the loss of everything people believed in, and because they recognized the triumph of nihilism, the triumph of meaninglessness, they were able to fill the void with the lies that worked because they responded to a basic desire: everything is rotten, reform is a waste of time, let's destroy everything. Hence, Arendt suggests that fascism has added a new version of the ancient art of lying: lying the truth.

One of the issues that we have all grappled with in recent years in Israel is how someone like Netanyahu can be viewed as an uncommon liar by some and an unusual truth-teller by others. Arendt would explain this paradox that he is, in a sense, "lying the truth." That does not imply that he is a fascist or a totalitarian. Rather, he is someone who has a genuine grasp of and control over that vacuum. The desire for destruction is driven by the conviction that the whole system is rotten, hypocritical, and unjustified, and therefore more than rescuing or repairing it, it must be destroyed. When this is realized, public relations can be used to mobilize a kind of lie that looks like a true story. The insight that emerges from Arendt's remarks is that if you tell people that the system is rotten, screwed up, even if you lie, the audience will not care, because you really hold on to the depths of things.

Of course, there is a yearning for destruction on the left as well. In general, there is a lot of rage out there these days. Aside from worldwide conspiracy ideas about capitalists, the rage recently included frustration with the coronavirus, claiming that people are using it to bring about other preplanned economic and social changes. However, more conservatives believe that the state of Israel is so corrupt and decadent that it is preferable to destroy it than to change it. And it is this "nihilistic notion" that fills the void they have created. Although opinions differ, it is the same vacuum that Arendt described as existing in Europe at the time. In Israel, left-wing populism still dominates many cultural institutions. And there are individuals on the right who advocate for culture's abolition on the grounds that it is "leftist" and "white." Netanyahu is one among them. He cancels anyone who says or does something he doesn't like. He refers to his supporters as "real Jews." The latter retaliates by directing its militancy and chauvinism at "Jews who have forgotten what it means to be Jewish." Their battle cry is "leftists," a disparaging epithet that has become a symbol of a fictitious foe—the elitist logos. The peripherial right wing's animosity toward Israel's historic social-cultural center is a symptom of nihilism, that is, it is unrelated to politics. The danger with nihilism is that, while construction is born out of a search for common interests that leads to alliances and compromises with people we disagree with, nihilism makes people feel lonely, swept away, and out of touch with reality. As a result, rather than seeking compromises and agreements, they seek something that will make them feel complete, which leads to a destructive mindset.

CHAPTER 5

Reflections on Politics and Revolution in Light of the Student Uprising in the 1960s

THE LAST ARTICLE IN *Crises of the Republic* is actually an adaptation of one of Arendt's late interviews in German conducted by journalist Edelbert Reif in 1970, in which Arendt was asked to clarify and elaborate on a few points raised in the article on violence. In fact, it can be viewed as an extension and interpretation of the previous article on violence. Her thoughts here continue topics such as "revolutionary situation," "real analysis of the existing situation," Marxism and capitalism, and the alternative she proposes to the concept of the nation-state and the degeneration of the representative system, namely the principle of federation and direct democracy's local self-government. This can be considered her life-long ideal for which she spent so much thought on the meaning of revolution.

The first part of the interview deals with political protest. Her insights here on the student revolt sum up the discussions from the previous two articles on what it means to take part in practical political action. Arendt's critique of the revolutions is a continuation of her critique of violence in the previous article. We have seen that violence silences power. Politics is based on speech and persuasion, but a person falls silent when a gun is aimed at him.

That is why violence destroys politics. Arendt's reflections here are related to the fact that she thinks of power in a positive way, that is, as a political action in which citizens can participate in the political process.

In the article on violence, Arendt's impression of the student revolt is equivocal. She recognizes good things: it is a global movement, with differences from country to country, though their common ground is the confidence that things can be changed by their efforts. Specifically for America, compared to the "quiet generation" of the fifties, who were more interested in cars than politics, Arendt was impressed by the involvement of the generation of the sixties in protest against the war, the demand for freedom of speech, and the fact that they joined the human rights movements, which advocated equality, a fair wage for university staff, and the right to participate in the management of universities and to be given a break from studies in order to be involved in the election process. Apart from the morality of this generation, they discovered what in the eighteenth century was called "public happiness." That is, the entrance to public life is an expression of freedom; people are not forced to participate in this action, and thus it should be an activity with joy, something we do together with others, and thus create public happiness. Yet these achievements did not last long before they were wasted by fanaticism, unnecessary violence and destruction on the border of crime, adherence to ideologies, and boredom.

Therefore, to the interviewer's question about the hope of Ernest Bloch—one of the spiritual teachers of the German student movement—for an approaching revolution, Arendt argues that according to our historical experience since the eighteenth-century revolutions, there are some phenomena that belong to preconditions for an authentic revolution; for example, the loss of public trust in government and the failure of public services is a clear sign of the loss of the power of authority of the governments of the great powers. This is clearly seen in the light of a huge accumulation of means of violence by governments, although an increase in the amount of weapons cannot compensate for the loss of power. And on the part of the revolutionaries, as we have said, the moral factor has always been present. The history of revolutions also shows that it was not the oppressed who perpetrated them but those who could not bear the oppression of others. The political circumstances surrounding the revolution are thus authentic, in the sense that all of this represents what Arendt refers to as a "revolutionary situation." But this should not necessarily lead to a revolution. It could end in a counterrevolution, that is, the establishment of a tyrannical regime, or nothing. No one today knows anything about a revolution coming soon, and Bloch's principle of hope does not help us much. Arendt believes that the only way to establish freedom and authority in the modern world is through revolution. It is not simply a liberation but the foundation of freedom.

What does it take to start a revolution that will establish this freedom? According to Arendt, this is something that is revealed during the revolution itself. But she does want to say that, historically, revolutionaries themselves have never led to a revolution. What can pave the way for a revolution is what she calls a "real analysis of the existing situation." The meaning of this ambiguous concept becomes clearer here than elsewhere: people bring up a salad of ideologies that are clichés, such as Marxism, capitalism, anti-capitalism, and the union of the West with the "third world" (Sartre, Marcuse), that is, ideas that are mostly unreal to the situation, that do not turn to "what is." For the imperialists, Egypt and India are the same things—both fall into the definition of subject races. The new left mimics the imperialist comparison of all differences and only replaces the labels, thus continuing the unwillingness to see things as they are in reality without dressing up categories in an attempt to catalogue them. This is what led to their theoretical helplessness. The slogan "Former Colonial Natives in Undeveloped Countries—Unite!" is even crazier than the Marxist source it imitates: "Workers of the world—unite!" Which has already been proven unreliable. A true revolutionary is one who analyzes the existing situation in such a way that what he says will speak the truth to enough people in a way that will persuade them to join the revolution.

Thus, those who called themselves revolutionaries in the sixties did not realize that one does not need only a revolution but also the readiness and ability to pick up the power that lies in the streets. Their theoretical sterility and dim analysis were similar to that of the movement in Germany, where theoretical discourse is loved. Apart from shouting slogans and riots in the streets, the German students did not organize anything practical. In both America and Germany, the students gossiped about absolute ideas and categories from the nineteenth century. None of this was related to current conditions.

THE CRITICISM AGAINST THE UNIVERSITY

When asked if students in the United States are frustrated, Arendt responds that the student riots were not caused by frustration. Rather, the movement has made significant progress on the issue of African Americans and the Vietnam War. This success, however, could be squandered if they succeed in destroying the universities. In America, it is less of a problem because students have a more political orientation and less interest in the internal problems of the academy, and in fact, a large proportion of the students feel solidarity with the academy on substantive issues. But even there the university can be destroyed by the riots surrounding the crisis of faith in science and progress, which is not a political issue that affects the whole nation. The academy allows these young people to live free for several years without any obligations to society. If they destroy academia, they will lose that freedom, and with it, the possibility of criticism against society. In other places (like France and Germany) students have started sawing the branch on which they sit, and this "is connected with running amok."[1] In contrast, Eastern European students do not rebel at university and enjoy broad social support.

1. Arendt, *Crises of the Republic*, 170.

CAPITALISM AND SOCIALISM

In the previous article, Arendt discussed students' adherence to Marxist ideology in the context of violence, which begs the question, what does she think of capitalism and socialism per se? And she has a lot to say about it here. Almost all of her writings contain criticisms of Marxism's anti-political determinism. But her critical discussion of capitalism here stands out more than anywhere else. Her position here corresponds with her lengthy statistical-economic analysis of the modern crisis in *The Human Condition*: socialism and capitalism are equally problematic. The difference is that here she makes the same claim in the context of her "real analysis of the existing situation," namely the loss of power of governments today.

To the interviewer's question about the theoretical discourse that still deals with the idea of the historical development of humanity, for which there are only two possibilities—capitalism or socialism—Arendt argues that in "the real analysis of the existing situation," in both capitalist and socialist countries, the power of authority was lost for the same reason, namely the countries deprived their peoples of their private property, the first through taxation and the latter through secret police. In other words, they deprived the power of their peoples, their freedom.

Socialism and capitalism cannot be substituted for one another because they are twins who wear different hats. Both have a negative impact on the private sphere.

Arendt supposedly asks the students who imagine things about socialism in their playfulness with Marxist ideologies and Maoism, all the way up to Che Guevara and Fidel Castro, showing that socialism did indeed continue to the end of what capitalism began: Why see it as redemption? She adds that this is likely why the reform movements in the East haven't presented a better capitalist alternative to the model they're criticizing, because they all know capitalism can't replace socialism.

In conclusion, the competition is not between economic methods. Only when a dictator prevents the economy from being as productive as it would be without him, is the economic system relevant. The rest is a political question: What kind of state do we want, what constitution, law, in short, what protections do we get—whether it is guaranteed by a bourgeois government's law or by a communist state?

And to what extent is the idea of the welfare state a solution to the capital-government phenomenon?

WELFARE STATE

In their pure form, communism and socialism destroyed the working class, its institutions, unions, and parties, and its rights such as collective bargaining, strikes, unemployment benefits, and social security. In their place, these regimes offered the illusion that factories were working-class property—which has long since been destroyed—and the lie that unemployment does not exist—a lie based on the lack of unemployment benefits. Capitalists deprived the people of the ability to act significantly in public by impoverishing them, in part through overtaxation. Thus, although the students' moral approach to this problem is "revolutionary correct," looking at this situation from the point of view of the oppressed will not help here.

Capitalism destroyed the structure of feudal society: private assets, corporations, and guilds. It eliminated all the collective groups that constituted protection for the individual and his property, that is, that guaranteed his relative security, and placed in their place two classes: exploiters and exploited. Because the working class is essentially a collective, it still provides the individual with some protection, and after he has learned to organize, he struggles to secure workers' rights.

The idea of a republic was, for Arendt, an ideal that towered beyond socialism and capitalism. In her view, rational economic development devoid of ideology is possible. The way to a solution is not to dispossess the dispossessors but to find a way to manage matters so that the masses dispossessed by the systems in the socialist society and in the capitalist industrial society can accumulate property again.

The point here is that freedom is not just whether the citizen is allowed to say and print what he wants, or not. Or if my neighbors are spying on me, or not. Freedom always includes freedom to dissent. In other words, Arendt is concerned about the rise of the government as an economic player. A separation between economy and government is required: the threat of capital-government alliance on the private sphere must be confronted, and instead of the labels "capitalist" and "socialist" countries, one must think in the direction of countries that respect workers' rights, such as Sweden, and those who do not—such as the U.S., U.S.S.R., and Spain. We repeatedly rely on the traditional right-left socialism-capitalism standards to judge reality. And that's a mistake. We must rely on our judgment. And this is what Arendt's last book *The Life of the Mind* is all about.

Arendt does support the idea of a welfare state, whether in a socialist or capitalist form. Yet she had a different conception of well-being than ours today. In her opinion, the meaning of welfare is a concern for the basic needs of life. And it ends there. Just as capitalism and economic power are dangerous to freedom, so is government power when it is driven by economic and social concerns. And this is one of the recurring themes throughout her work, especially in the book *The Human Condition*. The concept of "The Rise of the Social" means a modern phenomenon of the emergence of another domain other than (the traditional) private and public spheres, which destroyed both and, in fact, destroyed politics, because politics are supposed to be exercised in public space. And thus Arendt suspects that the expansion of the administrative system's force in the welfare state is as dangerous as capitalism.

TOWARDS MORE HUMANE SOCIALISM?

Since, according to Arendt, capitalism is not an alternative to socialism, the interviewer asks her about the prospect of a more humanistic "democratic socialism" in satellite countries in the East. By the time of the interview here (1970), Arendt assumed that such attempts would appear here and there if the powers would leave them in peace. It is difficult to predict what it looks like in a field like the economy, but it will certainly focus on the issue of property ownership. In East Germany, for example, they are trying a cooperative method that is not derived from socialism, which has proven itself in Denmark and Israel. And in Yugoslavia, they are trying a method of self-management in factories, a new version of the old workers' councils, which by chance are not part of the communist orthodox socialist doctrine. The "councils" are the only real consequence of the revolutions—as opposed to the revolutionary and ideological parties. In any case, according to Arendt, the positive common denominator in these attempts is that they are not related to a particular economic system but only to the principle that an economic system must not deprive people of their freedom. The U.S.S.R. has an interest in intervening in a satellite countries when such economic attempts join the struggle for freedom, for fear that one of these countries will flee the Warsaw Pact.

Although the discussion here of Soviet communism is irrelevant today, Arendt's conclusions about "socialist humanism"—the attempt to undo the inhumanity that socialism brought about without the need to present a capitalist system—are still relevant to Russian centralism in Putin's era. In Arendt's opinion at the time of the interview, there was a chance that such attempts would work in small countries, as in the case of Yugoslavia and Czechoslovakia (or Romania and Hungary), whether they call themselves socialists or not. But for the great powers, it is problematic because the mass societies have gotten out of control, that is, the ability to rule over them. Another factor to consider is that the U.S.S.R. and satellite countries are not nation-states but made up of different nations. In each of them, the government is in the hands of the more dominant nation than the rest, and its opposition is in constant danger of falling into a liberation movement. Especially in Russia, the dictators are more afraid of the collapse of the Russian Empire than of a change in government. That is, the concern here is not socialism but political power, as it always has been.

To conclude the discussion on socialism and capitalism, Arendt is asked if anti-Bolshevism is stupidity. And she repeats what she said about the "ideologists" in the article on lying in politics. Specifically, it is an invention of those who believed in Stalin and one day awoke from the illusion to seek a new god, and even the polar opposite: Satan. They simply replace the thought pattern. But it is ironic to say that instead of looking for beliefs, they see reality. Whether these anti-Bolsheviks see the devil in the East or the Bolsheviks see the devil in the United States, it's the same mentality: to see black and white.

Towards the end of the interview, Arendt emphasizes an important point from the article on violence: where government power is dwindling, it does not resist the temptation to replace it with violence. In all the republics with representative governments, the people delegated power to some people to act on their behalf. Loss of the state's power marks the withdrawal of the people from agreeing on what their representatives are doing. Obviously, those who have received power feel powerful. Even after the people have dropped their base, their sense of power remains. That is, persons who have received "power" begin to act as rulers and replace the consent between government and the people with "force." And this is a turning point, as in the case of the Vietnam War that not only split the public but caused a lack of trust in the system per se and thus a loss of power. It created a "credibility gap," which means a lack of faith in people in positions of power regardless of whether they agree with them or not. Since the Tonkin Bay incident, the Vietnam War has been widely perceived as not only inhuman or immoral but illegal. And it has a heavier weight in America than in Europe where the public does not believe its politicians in advance. The question that interests Arendt here is how an illegal war gained widespread support among the American public. This brings us back to the issue of the conduct of the student resistance movement.

WORKING-CLASS SUPPORT FOR MILITARY INTERVENTION IN VIETNAM

Arendt explains that in the U.S. the opposition's first impetus to the war came from universities, especially white students, that is, from those groups that took part in the civil rights movement. This opposition was aimed from the beginning against "the system" whose most loyal supporters to date are the workers, that is, the low-income sector. According to Arendt, middle- and lower-class whites in America have good reason to believe that all the reforms for African Americans were done at their expense. For example, in the big cities, the free public school system has collapsed under the weight of the almost absolute majority of proletarian African Americans who have lowered the standard of living and studies due to poor education at home for discipline and lack of basic education. According to working-class whites, elitist upper-middle-class liberals are unwilling to pay the price and send their children to private schools or move to expensive suburbs. In this view, the white proletariat's support for the war expresses its distaste for any elite and including the students. And more generally, Marx did say that the proletariat has no state. But the proletariat never agreed with this view. The lower classes everywhere are particularly prone to nationalism, chauvinism, and imperialist policies. But according to Arendt, specifically in America, there was another reason, which was reflected in the split of the civil rights movement into blacks and whites as a result of the war. White students from good middle-class families joined the movement immediately, while African Americans, following their leaders (including Martin Luther King), suspended their decision to demonstrate against the war due to the fact that the army was opening up educational and professional possibilities for the lower class.

In this context, Arendt notes that despite the "sin of ideology" of the student movements in the West, white Americans at least posed questions that concerned the whole nation. This is in contrast to the student movement in Germany (SDS) which has relished theoretical nonsense flourishing in the air—for example, their preoccupation with visiting Eastern rulers like the Persian Shah. They had an ardent interest in international affairs that did not involve risk and responsibility, an interest that was usually a cover-up for concealing realistic national interests, such as some crucial international issues in which Germany could play an important role after the war, including some moral questions. Similar to the question of why would a lower-class American—whose army is his source of livelihood—oppose war, one may ask here why would a German worker who has achieved a comfortable material standard of living care about some war in Southeast Asia?

And here it is important to add a brief summary due to all the talk about universities here and in the previous article. Will the revolution come from the workers or from the elites? Arendt was concerned that the working class and the elites were not talking to each other. And this failure is related, in her opinion, to the intellectual side of the matter. Even when the intellectual elites speak on behalf of the working class, they will not listen to them. And this was also very topical in the wave of protests in Israel. The student movements in the sixties were too committed to the ideology of the left wing, which prevented them from seeing the world as it was. It seems that even today, the academy is infected with the takeover of elites with a certain ideology, for example, identity politics, which excludes others. At the same time, in the article on violence, Arendt regrets the tendency to blame politicization solely on the actions of disobedient students, because it was the establishment of universities that began this through their dependence on men of power, which made them—as Henry Steele put it—"the government's manpower agency." Here, as in all of her writings, Arendt sometimes says we must think about what we do, and at other times she says we must say "what is." And "say what is" means not being ideological, not taking one side, because then you do not say "what" is but what is in the context of one political point of view.[2] Arendt has revolutionary reasons to think that the only

2. Arendt saw herself committed only to reality. However, this position became problematic in her book *Eichmann in Jerusalem* because of her opposition to the notion that Jews can be only victims. She thought that the Jewish claim that the Holocaust was ideological was not "true."

way to create a revolution is to push for a nonideological search for truth in order to say what is there, and this requires de-politicizing universities into a system with true openness of thought.

ARENDT'S OWN ANALYSIS OF THE EXISTING SITUATION

The last part of the interview returns to the issue of "the real analysis of the existing situation," a point that links us to Lenin's question: "What is to be done?" One can imagine the young Lenin and some of his student friends sitting in a room and contemplating on what can be done in front of mighty power. For Arendt, the fact that the criminal governments have now lost their power, and it is scattered in the streets, is only the initial analysis of the situation. The challenge is, how do we create and establish from this power new methods of power that are not tyrannical? Essentially, Arendt does not think of another idea of a state but of changing the form of the present one. In the article on violence she argued that as long as there are sovereign nation-states, world peace is a utopia. Because the meaning of sovereignty and state as we know it since the fifteenth and sixteenth centuries is that international conflicts can be resolved only through war, and as we have seen today, war is no longer a possibility because of the monstrous development of instruments of violence, we therefore require a new idea.

As a conclusion from the Eichmann trial, Arendt claims that a practical power is needed over the states that will respond when necessary to "radical evil" such as genocide. This is not about establishing a better international court than the one in The Hague, or a new League of Nations that will recycle the same nation-state conflict within it. Supernational authority will be ineffective because the dominant state within it will take over, leading to a world government and ultimately to the most dangerous tyranny that there is no escape from—a global police force. The final solution here is not supernational but international. The ultimate question is: where are the models that will help us interpret, at least theoretically, the "international authority" at its peak of control?[3] How can what is supreme also be "between"?

THE FEDERAL PRINCIPLE AND COUNCIL SYSTEM

According to Arendt, the first elements of the new state idea are in the federal system whose advantage is that power does not move from above or below but horizontally so that there is mutual supervision of the federal units.[4] The federal principle will combine a second idea, namely "council system"—small, egalitarian, spontaneous, popular, voluntary associations that emerged throughout the country during the French and American Revolutions, as well as the revolutions in the twentieth century up until the Hungarian uprising of 1956 against the influence of the U.S.S.R.[5] The point

3. Arendt, *Crises of the Republic*, 187–88.

4. Arendt, *Crises of the Republic*, 188. During and immediately after World War II, Arendt wrote extensively on federations, such as on how Europe should be a federation, and also in the context of Palestine. However, she realized in 1945 that power wants to grow. It was a Nietzschean idea. And she thinks the American Constitution understood this and tried to create as many barriers to the concentration of power. As mentioned, at the end of *On Revolution* she claims that it failed and the proof of this today is the dangerous rise of the US federal government. At the same time, she saw nationalism as Europe's problem that its solution is a kind of European federalism that will bring freedom and protection from a centralist government. But in her opinion, Russia will not allow Europe to become a federal state because it wants to control it. "Power" in the sense of "force" is the motive of politics.

5. The October Revolution in Russia and the uprising in Hungary in 1956 saw spontaneous councils (workers, artists, etc.) formed for the purpose of establishing a political body with a new form of government and developed in coordination with a federation until the election of representatives to a national council, in a North American style. According to Arendt, modern revolutions brought to the forefront the experience of freedom, which had been new since the fall of the Roman Empire. And for those who brought about the revolution, it was also an experience of discovering the human ability to start something new. And that was at the heart of the pathos of the American and French Revolutions: the stubbornness of never having been so great and significant in all of human history. Only in the presence of this pathos of innovation, when it is linked to the idea of freedom, can one speak of a revolution. Common to the premodern uprisings and the revolution is that they appear

here is to disperse the power in order to try to get people to participate in institutions so that they have more direct power in making policy decisions that affect their lives.

Although the council system was always and everywhere, destroyed whether directly by the bureaucracy of the nation-states or by the party machines,[6] in Arendt's view this is the only alternative that has appeared in history time and again. Even if it is utopian, at least it is a utopia of the people and not of theorists and ideologies.[7] In this model of government that stems from and

through violence, which is the reason for the confusion between them. But only where change takes place in the sense of a new beginning, where violence is used to form a different form of government to bring about the formulation of a new political body, where liberation at least means the establishment of freedom—one can speak of revolution (Arendt, *On Revolution*, 26–28). On another occasion, it would be interesting to compare the approaches of Arendt and the French philosopher and political activist Simone Weil (1909–1943), to the idea of revolution. I will only note here that together with the common sides in their cultural critique, for example, the combination of appreciation and critique of Marx, and the Stalinist distortion of the communist idea in the U.S.S.R. and the flaws of capitalism, according to Weil, the nature of society condemns it to a relationship of control and domination, and therefore the idea of revolution is an illusion. No matter who seizes power, there will always be perpetrators and commanders, because it is impossible to govern and work in manual labor at the same time. The only solution to the oppression of working conditions is to add a spiritual dimension to the process by connecting the worker to religious symbols that will give meaning to his life—a connection between his thoughts and his actions. But as stated, Arendt denies transcendence (metaphysics) and religious purposes. For her, there is only one world, and there is no point in life other than becoming politically free—and thus happy—through participatory democracy, which will limit the arbitrariness of giving instructions from above. This form of government, which leaves room for human capacity for a new beginning, is made possible only by revolution.

6. For example, Lenin saw the councils as temporary instruments during the revolution. And a revolution is meant to attain power, which means ownership of the means of violence. And like Robespierre before him, he too eliminated them, because they threatened the Bolshevik Party's monopoly of power. Therefore his slogan "All power to the Soviets" and the name after the October Revolution "Soviet Union" are a lie that covered the popularity of a single party that made the Soviet system impotent (Arendt, *On Revolution*, 261–62).

7. According to Arendt, not only the historians and political theorists who supported the revolutions, but even the revolutionary tradition itself failed to understand the innovation brought by the councils, which Jefferson called

corresponds with the very experience of political action, one can find a completely different type of organization that starts from the bottom, continues up, and finally leads to the parliament. And to avoid misunderstandings, Arendt remarks that the hippies and dropouts of all kinds have nothing to do with it. On the contrary, their basis is a denial for all public life and politics in general. At the same time, as survivors of shipwrecked politics, their style is justified for personal reasons. Arendt sees in their style, in Germany and America, something grotesque, but she understands and accepts them. But politically they are meaningless. The councils aspire just the opposite. There are different types of councils such as neighborhood councils, professional councils, factories, apartment houses, artists' councils in cafes, but their message is simple: the right to participate, to argue, to make your voice heard in public, and shape the country's political path. Arendt is aware of the fact that the state is too large to gather all the residents in one room to define their fate. Therefore we need free public spaces.

The compartment in which we deposit the ballots is too small, containing only one person. And we have already said that the parties are not suitable unless we all choose to be manipulated. But even if only ten of us have sat around a table, each expressing his opinion and listening to the opinions of others, a rational form can be obtained through an exchange of opinions. From such a discussion it will soon become clear who deserves to represent them towards the higher council, where the opinions will be revised again from the incandescence of a variety of opinions. Not every citizen should be a member of such councils. Not everyone

---

"elementary republics," as an out-of-parliament resistance force with a new form of government and a public space that gives expression to the voice of all (Arendt, *On Revolution*, 252–53). The revolutions of the twentieth century were carried out with advance preparation in a scientific style by professional revolutionaries. Their model is a single party that fought the spontaneity of the councils to land them in the rank of temporary instrument, a romantic dream. The members of these councils did not identify with any party or with what was about to become a party (Arendt, *On Revolution*, 266–67). In fact, the party system today is a continuation of the same one-party model, in that it does not represent the opinion of the citizens but is a force that "cartels" and controls their power (Arendt, *On Revolution*, 273).

wants to worry about public affairs. But that means that decisions that concern him will be taken without him. But the opportunity must be open to everyone. In any case, this way, a process of self-selection must begin that will produce a true political elite.[8] This is the direction in which Arendt sees an opportunity to create a new idea of a state. A council-state of this kind, to which the principle of sovereignty would be completely foreign,[9] would be perfectly

8. The fact that modern parties have allowed—in the spirit of modern equality—for the lower class to climb socially does not mean that they have allowed citizens as a people to participate in the political process. The elite that grew from below only replaced the wealth and inheritance elite of the premodern era, because the relationship between those in power in the public sphere and those in the darkness of the private sphere remained the same. There is no legitimate growth of an elite out of action in concert of citizens in the public sphere. Politician became a profession according to the party's standards, and therefore it is rare for talented people to survive the apparatus—although the federation creates a pyramid, too, but not of an authoritarian government, because each stage is supported not from above or below but by its rank. The elite of councilors will be composed at least of those who put the good of the republic before their personal happiness (Arendt, *On Revolution*, 281–84). From an Arendtian point of view, to be honest, most people do not want to be engaged in politics. And those who do want to participate in the councils and have something to say and the means and talent for it will go up and gain persuasive power and influence. But it is better that we have a political elite that is based on participation and a desire to be involved than one that is based on "save me, and I will save you" as is customary in a representative system. That is, we must accept the elitism of a minority that runs politics as long as the system is open to all, no one is excluded, and elite people rise in the merit of their actions and participation rather than because they bought the entrance or were put in by someone.

9. Arendt saw local councils and the federation as the only formula for preventing totalitarianism (Arendt, *On Revolution*, 283). She tried to formulate a political solution for stateless people, a problem she herself had suffered from as a Jew for a decade since the Nazis came to power. Such a solution must presuppose a separation between state and nation and prevent the nation from taking over the state, since in the modern age the granting of rights is done by the state. She was impressed by the American model because the U.S. is an immigrant state in which basically anyone can take part. That is, the "right to rights" is not based on particular origin but on more universal standards (letter to Jaspers, June 30, 1947, in Arendt and Jaspers, *Hannah Arendt-Karl Jaspers*, 90–91). In other words, the anti-Semitism she experienced as an outcast from Nazi Germany and the mainstream of Zionism led to her opposition to the idea of nationalism. In her opinion, the political solution

suited to federations of various kinds, chiefly because power is established horizontally rather than vertically. Regarding the prospect of a revolution in the late sixties, Arendt replied: little. But maybe in the next revolution.[10]

---

for Jews is the establishment of a homeland that will not fall into a nation-state, such as the Jewish settlement in Palestine before the establishment of the state that fulfilled a Jewish political ideal that allowed Jewish culture to flourish without the need for sovereignty. At first, she expressed concern and even support for Israel, because she saw Zionism as the only serious political attempt to deal with anti-Semitism, but began to move away from Zionism due to the strengthening of political (Herzliyan) Zionism and the identification between Zionism and the aspiration for a nation state. Sovereign collective self-determination—which was Ben Gurion's main vision—would lead to the power control of one nation over other ethnic minorities. In the forties, she came under very harsh criticism of the Mapai establishment led by Ben Gurion in a series of articles, the most notable of which was *Zionism Reconsidered* (1945). The fact that they established a state does not mean that things work. Instead of a two-state solution, she suggested in these articles a model of a Jewish-Arab federation composed of jointly managed local councils, which would be expanded later on throughout the entire Middle East. However, as part of her work with the *Aliyat Hano'ar* (at the time, she worked for the World Zionist Organization in Paris in the thirties), she visited Palestine and gained a good acquaintance with the kibbutzim. Of all the Zionist enterprises, she valued only the kibbutz (and the Hebrew University), which constitute perhaps the most promising of all social experiments made in the twentieth century, as well as the most magnificent part of the Jewish homeland, which in her opinion gives hope in the face of modern crisis like the phenomenon of mass society (Arendt, *Jewish Writings*, 395). During the Six-Day War (June 5–10, 1967), she suddenly expressed enthusiastic support for Israel, arguing that it was a just war. In any case, Arendt's approach to Zionism has recently gained renewed interest among new Israeli historians.

10. Arendt, *Crises of the Republic*, 189–91. Arendt thought there was no way out of the situation we are in but a revolution. Hence she also says in a somewhat less optimistic tone that the only compensation for the loss of the "treasure" from the revolutions—namely the spirit of starting something new, which has not found an institution to preserve it—is a memory in which poets excel. For example, the Frenchman Char, who joined the resistance in the war, wrote about the experience of finding his true self at that time, as opposed to the boring and depressing public life of the post-war routine (Arendt, *On Revolution*, 284–85).

CONCLUSION

The main problem today is centralism. The growing lack of public trust in governments is related, on the one hand, to the rise of authoritarian regimes that have replaced power with violence which always turns into terrorism. On the other hand, the solution of liberal democratic welfare states to their inability to govern due to the size of governments and populations and the collapse of the civil service is control by a repressive administration. The degeneration of the representative system—the inability of elected officials to truly represent the electorate who put them in power—only accelerated the bureaucratization of political life ("nobody's rule"), leading to the elimination of the relationship between government and citizen, which in turn leads to an increase in violence in society. In this respect, capitalism and socialism are equally flawed. There is no doubt that the steady increase in the centralization of power in the United States that Arendt spoke of parallels the direction that the state of Israel has taken under Netanyahu's regime. The problem is that it weakens ordinary people while strengthening those at the center, the rulers, who "know better."[11] In fact, sometimes it is more just to strengthen the position of the minority against the wrong position of the masses. There are beloved dictators. The right-wing newspapers in Israel still praise Netanyahu as the one who went into opposition as Israel's most popular politician. Sometimes there are advantages to living under a tyrannical regime when there is a generous dictator. But once the public decides to go in that direction, even if for good reasons, according to Arendt, it empowers a regime that is able to make decisions without the participation of the majority of the public, which ends up pursuing goals by means that most of us do not like. We have seen this recently in the U.S. when the federal government under Trump became an uncontrollable bureaucratic actor that often did

---

11. In Arendt's opinion, these two movements of centralization are dangerous; and right-wing populism, whose power is intensifying in the world and in Israel, usually has a tendency toward both.

not take into account other positions and points of view, which was also the case during the Netanyahu administration.

One of the issues at the heart of recent election campaigns in the U.S. and Israel has been government corruption. The question arises, however, of what guarantees that a leadership that opposes this corruption—as Arendt sees it in the councils of a state—will be pure of it, when it comes to power? One of the few things Arendt urges us to do is to accept things as they are. People act out of various interests that are more or less important, but they all exist. And there will always be corruption at all levels. Arendt's point is not to change human nature. That's what it is. The book *The Human Condition* is called that because the question of "human nature" is unanswered in politics. Finding something like that is like jumping over our own shadow. Maybe God can know what it is and define it, because he created man. All one has to look for when thinking about politics are the conditions that influenced people at a particular time to favor such foci over others, and that is the "human condition," according to Arendt's political theory.[12] We can indeed provide role models of pure-minded people in the hope that they will inspire people to act as they do. But that will not happen on a large scale.[13] So the point is to create government structures that neutralize the effects of corruption as much as possible by creating multiple sources of power, so that when one becomes corrupt, the others step in and oppose it. And if they, too, are corrupted, others will stand against them. Because of the structure of the American Constitution and government, Arendt

12. This assumption that the crisis of modernity is in man and not in the world dominates the social sciences and psychology. Their entire analysis of what is happening in the world deals with behaviorism that ignores the fact that man is an agent of action that produces events in the world (Kohn, *Promise of Politics*, 107).

13. For example, in the book *Men in Dark Times*, Arendt describes a mosaic of characters such as Walter Benjamin, Karl Jaspers, Ephraim Lessing, and Rosa Luxemburg who demonstrated judgment in objective conditions hostile to freedom of thought. That is, in the "dark times" of the twentieth century when the light of public sphere was obscured by "invisible governments," we achieved enlightenment from these individuals who left us with a sense that no matter how horrible things may be, they can be different too.

was less concerned about the corruption of politicians. However, right-wing demagoguery has infiltrated nihilism into politics: the lie of truth, which has to do with the corruption of people who prefer lies to reality. The danger Arendt fears in America, then, is not the corruption of officials but the corruption of the people—when people are more interested in their private interests than in public concerns, that is, when they leave politics in the hands of a corrupt elite, so to speak. Arendt proposes to combat this corruption by providing institutional spaces for people to engage in public affairs. This is why councils and town halls are so important to her. It is not about councils always being good and always doing the right thing, nor does the number of participants matter. What matters is that the rooms are there and available for those who choose to go there and participate. Even if citizens do not come, the institutions will remain. Arendt truly believes that institutions are important and that they must be created if we take into account the fact that people are sometimes corrupt and imperfect.[14]

14. According to Arendt, the drafters of the American Constitution succeeded in securing the republic from the emergence of tyranny through brakes like the separation of powers. The threat to an egalitarian society is precisely the corruption of the bureaucracy, not on the part of the elected representatives, but rather from the people from whom the officials who instill private interests in public affairs emerge (Arendt, *On Revolution*, 255–56). In an early article Arendt tried to understand what motivated people to turn screws into a mighty machine for mass murder. She explains that Himmler believed in the kind of decency that he maintained for the German family and built his terrorist organization on the idea of a respectable and decent bourgeoisie. In his diabolical genius he turned family members into mass murderers. According to Arendt, the bourgeoisie is not a German but a modern problem. It sees no concern for any civil society, culture, or value, but only for personal progress and livelihood, to preserve family life (Kohn, *Essays in Understanding*, 128–29). And later in the book *The Origins of Totalitarianism* she noted that the intellectual source on which Nazism is based is Thomas Hobbes, whom Arendt sees as the great philosopher of the bourgeoisie. Hobbes perceives the person as someone who is no longer concerned with reason or the public, but with gaining power for himself. And in this pursuit of power there are obstacles that are other people. All people are equal, and even the weak can recruit people like him to defeat the strong. Hence the need for a judge to set rules for competition. And this judge is the state, the *Leviathan*. According to Hobbes, the last step of man is to place someone above him, the Leviathan

An important argument that runs like a thread through the book *Crises of the Republic* is the impact of the constitutional crisis that accompanies the process of centralization and the loss of governmental power. Most Western governments today have a separation of powers and institutional brakes that the Weimar Republic did not have when the Nazis came to power. In the United States, there are institutional brakes on anyone holding a position of power in the central federal government, such as Congress, the Supreme Court, states, districts, and councils. And in Israel, too, the Supreme Court demonstrates great vitality. But here, too, one must remain vigilant. In Arendt's view, the decline of its power is the great danger we face, as the article "Lying in Politics" shows. As long as constitutional power is respected in the country, it will be difficult for the state to fall into tyranny. As we have seen in the case of Trump and Netanyahu, demagogic authoritarian leaders around the world are trying to change their constitution, meaning they are working to trample and even obliterate some of these brakes: Brazil, Venezuela, Turkey. Precisely because of the limits of a constitution, one cannot be indifferent to the fact that someone will try to change it.[15]

That is why Arendt says in *On Revolution* that no constitutional law is enough to stop a power that decides to become absolute. Only power can control power. Power does not come from laws but from people acting together. This is why Arendt believes it is so important for people to be politically engaged, and why we need free political spaces where people act and build power when necessary, because this is the only way we can preserve freedom

who will allow him to empower his own power to control others, which is, according to Arendt a rejection of humanity, in the name of private interest.

15. According to Benjamin Wiker, every conservative today sympathizes with the fear of anti-federalists that national government will accumulate too much power. And we see a resurgence of this classic debate, with one difference, that today it seems that anti-federalists' fear that the power of the federal government will not complement but replace the local governments is a fulfilled prophecy. Nevertheless, anti-federalists today do not explicitly call for the dissolution of the Constitution. That is, like Arendt, Wiker recognizes that in the last hundred years these brakes have been hit in a way that frightens even federalists (Wiker, *10 Books*, 127–50).

and protect ourselves from tyranny, the potential of which we see emerging again today. As in the U.S., apart from Netanyahu's attacks on sources of power such as the Supreme Court and the police, we see a growing level of political activity by right-wing populists. The basic principles and virtues of the state of Israel are interpreted differently by the right and the left, and the right is more dangerous to democracy. The Israeli Supreme Court is a kind of equivalent to the U.S. Constitution. It is responsible for dealing with and preserving fundamental values such as justice, equality, pluralism, and more. Therefore, it must remain independent.[16] Right-wing populist journalists and intellectuals like to muddle through these fundamental values. The Kohelet Policy Forum research institute, for example, which works to shape the Israeli right according to national and libertarian views inspired by the right in the United States, simultaneously strives to influence the composition of the Supreme Court judges (in whatever way possible) in order to control their worldview. Whereas in America the founding fathers ensured that the Constitution could be amended only by the people, while to the government it is like the Bible—observe and sanctify—Israeli right-wing politicians seek to manipulate the core values upon which the state was founded. And the result is that a significant portion of the Israeli public rejects the basic democratic principles of the state. Similar to America, for example, a

16. The founding fathers in America separated the Constitution from the government, as we saw in the essay on civil disobedience. For them, it is the right of every nation to establish a constitution—it is the property of the people and not of the government—and guarantees its authority to restrict the government when necessary. For example, the fact that a government is partially elected does not mean that it is less tyrannical when elected officials gain unlimited power. And there is no better mechanism for overseeing government laws than a constitution. The constitution is open to changes at the initiative of the people according to the given circumstances, but out of preservation of its principled spirit. And no nation has a vested interest in making a mistake. And just as an heir does not have to use the entire inheritance, so each generation can decide for itself whether to adapt the constitution to its needs. Whereas for the government, the constitution is an inalienable law—a pocket Bible for every member of parliament—the government has no part in changing any section of the constitution.

large segment of the public is convinced that Netanyahu's election was stolen by a conspiracy.

A Life in Politics That Has Ceased to Be Politics

In an early book draft titled *Introduction Into Politics*,[17] Arendt asked whether politics has any meaning today. One of the discussions in the book is about the distinction between ends and goals, which are based on values. Both lie outside of politics and are independent of it. The goals (aspirations) of political action are guidelines that guide us in a world that cannot be defined in advance; they are not set in stone. And their fulfillment is constantly changing because we are dealing with other people who also have values and goals. Because there will never be complete freedom, there are always more people. In contrast, the ends are predefined. Once violence (brute force) enters the public sphere, goals become predefined ends, like a craft product in the Aristotelian sense, that is, the ultimate end justifies the means. The fact that it is rare for a political action to achieve its ambitions does not mean that it is meaningless, because it is not directed toward a clear unequivocal "point" (end) in the first place. The political goal depends on persuasion and negotiation in response to changing situations, that is, in a manner consistent with politics as human pluralism. The ends, on the other hand, are well defined, and therefore the means justify them: to achieve the absolute, one must destroy all the aspirations ("goals") and ideas of others. In this respect, promoting goals by violent means makes them ends.

Arendt argues in all her writings that politics is based on opinions, not truth. The collection of opinions creates meaning, even if it is not scientific. Meaning lies in political activity itself— the negotiation between goals (aspirations) and values. If politics is interested only in ends, it becomes meaningless, without depth.

Since the parties in the Israeli reality are unable to reach a minimal agreement on anything, it is an existential matter for

17. Originally written in German, first published (in English) as a long fragment in Jerome Kohn's collection *The Promise of Politics*.

them to destroy each other. And the means to that is to gain control outside of parliament by turning their electorate against each other. And so political action can be steered in various superficial directions that change from one day to the next—depending on fashion. So the idea that we can have politics that is based on values and depth, that we can have moral motives, is almost unimaginable today.[18] The only "meaning" that political action has is violence, coercion, even if the "end" is freedom. The confusion between ends and goals manifests itself in endless conflicts between political actors creating false representations detached from actual reality, leading historians, who are supposed to tell what happened (the factual truth), to fall into endless interpretive debates. The endless chatter that accompanies this is very present in the Israeli media.

To use Arendt's words, the question of government (the form of government) in Israel has been reduced to foreign policy in the sense of securing the borders. This means that there is actually no politics. And in an anti-political world, a "political desert" where politics is a war, we all need an oasis—the isolation of the artist, the solitude of the philosopher, solace with lovers and friends. But the danger lies in escapism, that is, a retreat not to judge and suffer but for comfort. An escape into a happy bourgeois life, an artist who paints without delving into an artistic process, or a philosopher who searches for answers without diving into questions.[19]

18. For example, a debate on the issue of state and religion. It seems that everything today has become a struggle for budgets; Orthodox politics is no longer related to Judaism in the deepest sense but to passions and lusts for dominion, like everyone else.

19. In light of Goethe's statement that poets do not commit serious sins and therefore unlike ordinary people should be forgiven—Arendt wondered how to relate to the sin of Bertold Brecht who was an apologist of Hitler and Stalin. Arendt appreciates artists; in the book *The Human Condition* she talks about how they build the political world because they put something in the world: painting, sculpture, song, and building. They say "what is there," and in doing so, they also make it a "thing" in our common world. Brecht was part of a generation living in disaster, dark times: the break in tradition, an anonymous mass society that sought identity and leadership and were led by the totalitarian movement. But he wrote about pirates and adventures. He was

According to Arendt, the human world is a product of love for the world, *amor mundi*. And the challenge of living in it is to affirm it, along with nihilism and horror. To ask the question of the unworldliness of the world is to deal with the profound anti-political character of our time. To ask what politics means today, then, is to engage with a politics that has ceased to be politics.

The Public Sphere

Is it correct to speak of a loss of the public sphere in Israel today? In general, the split in communication between right-wing and left-wing audiences seems to be due to the need for certainty, to the desire to read, see, and hear only what one believes oneself to be right. And so, for example, a right winger encounters left-wing opinions only through a right-wing populist journalist who trashes them. And so he never takes left-wing views seriously. Today we hardly see the press of the quarreling disputed groups talking to each other and developing common interests. And we have to take that into account when we think about democracy in Israel.[20]

Some say that the public sphere today takes place in the social networks. The question is what is discussed there and how they

---

endowed with a rare ability to say the unspeakable, to speak of joy, but he also joined the ranks of the Communist Party. And to be a communist in the third decade of the twentieth century was to forgive evil. He was willing to find excuses for Stalin for the murder of innocents in the name of "progress." And so he lied in that we can reconcile with reality. According to Arendt, in his poems and plays from that dark period, Brecht lost his "gift of poetry." That is to say, there is such a thing as inappropriate behavior of poets from Plato to Heidegger. At some point they need to acknowledge their guilt and take responsibility (Arendt, *Men in Dark Times*, 247–49). In the context of the protest in Israel, with the exception of artists like Assaf Amdursky, Achinoam Nini, and Arkadi Duchin, the majority of the performers exhibited questionable restraint. During the corona lockdown, Aviv Geffen, who cultivated the image of a "freedom warrior," met Netanyahu in person to elicit support.

20. Right wingers are afraid of change, and in their opinion, the left has made bad changes, while some on the left think the changes made by its governments as an agent of change are insufficient. These two groups are opposites, and it seems like this is going towards a civil war rather than a revolution.

are structured. Supposedly, communication via the internet allows people who normally had no public life to connect with each other, to talk to people. Suddenly they have a public life. With a click of a button, you can join any discussion on any topic on Zoom.[21]

21. Throughout his book *Public Sphere*, Habermas argues that in the eighteenth century existed what he calls a "bourgeois public sphere," that is, a dialogue between citizens through speech based on the recognition that citizens can agree on a common interest for all, if they accept the best rational argument; whereas in the democracy of post-World War II capitalism, this "communicative rationality" was disrupted by the intrusion of manipulative instrumental communication in which it is very difficult, if at all, to engage in rational discourse. This medium is dragging people into unenlightened decisions, the masses are fighting each other, each man for his private interest or his group. Habermas feared that public sphere was disappearing and believed in consensual communication through language aimed at freedom, versus technological rationale aimed at control.

For these reasons, he (and other communicators) saw Arendt as the one who placed the community at the heart of politics. In his view, her theory of action restores the dimension of a common goal that Aristotle argued was central to the formation of a political union.

But in Villa's view, neo-Kantians like Habermas were caught up in the "models" of the public sphere they found in her texts, which they took out of context and treated as normative ideals in a way that ignored the central argument in her book *The Human Condition*.

First, Arendt does not struggle with alienation per se between people (like Martin Buber, for example, in the book *I and Thou*), but with alienation to the world. She did not think we could revive the *agora* (market place of the ancient polis) through the resurrection of the intersubjective dimension through political group activity. More important for her is the renewal of our ability to resist the demand for "functional behavior" and to preserve as much as possible our ability to initiate agonistic action and independent and spontaneous judgment.

Second, for Arendt, there is no rational way to present a claim of truth or morality. In politics, all of these are opinions, and therefore they can be reconciled only through persuasion. Even if there is a common social factor that can be rationally defined, a public space of words and deeds is not a "dialogical communication" or a space for the fulfillment of moral goals (Kant), because when the aspiration is absent and all energy is directed to "truth," order, belonging, and solidarity, it becomes destructive. Arendt obviously appreciates rationalism but does not believe that the public sphere is its stage. The essence of political duty is not to ourselves or our community but to the world (Villa, *Arendt and Heidegger*, 205–6).

In the article "Lying in Politics," Arendt argued that when we deceive ourselves, we lose the stability necessary to coexist in a common political world. Fifty years later, the problem has grown astronomically and has become perhaps one of our greatest problems. The ability of people to live quietly in their intellectual world, whether online, in the academy (social sciences), or among friends, has led to a true de-factualization of the world.[22] Arendt explained that liars recognize what people are hungry for, and so they can construct a make-believe reality through the new advertising techniques. They build this illusory world through social media more than before, so we do not always know what and how it was built for us.

The Future of Political Life in Israel

The phenomenon of protest organizations has been a wonderful foundation for the creation of new sources of power, an example of political action of courageous spontaneous resistance to

22. Arendt was well aware of the impact of technology on politics. And she was concerned that if we don't think about what we are doing, we will become machines' slaves. But not in the way that some futurists believe the machines will communicate in order to take over the world. In *The Human Condition*, she argues that the telescope realized the human desire to escape from Earth and leave behind our biological and terrestrial boundaries by achieving an Archimedean point outside the Earth. We can recreate nature from this divine perspective if we want to live a longer, healthier, and faster life; a world with self-cleaning lakes; computers that feed and tutor children; more efficient cities; and so on. According to Arendt, this is not a scientific question, because there are already means to achieve it, but a political one: Do we really want it? Her point is that knowledge and thought have parted. We are no longer able to think rationally about what we do. We board a flight despite having no idea how the plane works. We became enslaved to computer technology in the sense that it speaks a mathematical language, i.e., a kind of universal sign system reserved for experts and incomprehensible to the general public. It replaced the language that allowed us to tell stories about the world and find collective meaning as a group. Today, in the age of social media, Arendt's question "Where are we when we think?" may be regarded as overly optimistic. Is there a private space left to think? Can we still be alone and converse with ourselves in the absence of all of our digital devices? What is the political value of being globally connected but unable to isolate ourselves from popular opinion?

control and violence in an atmosphere of glorification of violence by the right, and a bourgeoisie that pursues private interests that do not care about the concerns of the general public. The protest movement has created a model of public power that can survive a rupture of government arrangements. From a strict Arendtian perspective, the protest organizations did not recognize the "revolutionary situation" manifested in the Netanyahu government's loss of power, but their influence on public opinion was crucial to the coup. That is, they at least brought about reforms, like the students in France in the '68 revolt. The protest movement freed us from organized political crime, just as the settlers in America were freed from the English crown. According to Arendt, they were not truly free until they formed a government with spaces to participate. Unfortunately, that did not happen in Israel. The new Bennett-Lapid government is a dramatic step from the degeneration of democracy into the abyss. It has created a formidable opposition to the political demagoguery that has amassed too much power by making everyone around it and against it impotent. And it has presented a more horizontal form of power with the rotation model between prime ministers and the sharing of power with Israeli Arabs. It also has the possibility of restoring the power and prestige of veteran institutions such as the Supreme Court, which survived the onslaught of the Netanyahu government.

However, it is not a revolutionary government in the Arendtian sense, as I have stated. That is, it has nothing to do with the beginning of something new and with freedom, namely not with the question of the form of government.[23] Participation in public life, which Arendt defends, cannot be maintained through representative institutions,[24] and therefore the new government should

23. Arendt noted that when Jefferson learned about the uprising in Massachusetts while in Paris, he responded enthusiastically (in a letter to Colonel William Stephens Smith, Nov. 13, 1787): "We must not spend more than twenty years without such a revolt." The very fact that people stood up and acted was enough for him, no matter if the case was right or not, because "the tree of liberty needs to be refreshed from time to time with the blood of the patriots and tyrants. This is its fertilizing garbage" (Arendt, *On Revolution*, 236).

24. Benny Gantz's dramatic turnaround in the last round of the elections,

not be expected to rehabilitate the erosion of public services by bureaucracy. As long as mass society is ruled by the administration, violence in society will continue to increase. It won't bring back consensus, either, because only a revolution can give a political body a new common sense. As in the case of the uprising in the 1960s, the protest movement in Israel has not introduced a "new example" of politics. At most, there is a suspension of a solution, and as then, in Arendt's words, "we will have to wait for the next revolution."[25] And the implication that Israel is no longer a consensus society means that the new government must exist under the constant threat of right-wing populism from the opposition and its supporters—a public that lives in terrible disinformation—lurking around the corner.[26] In my discussion of political lies, we saw that the need for ideology was still essential in the sixties and seventies. The fact that the right in the State of Israel today speaks a language that proceeds from necessary historical patterns proves that it is essential here as well. And Arendt tells us that people who choose ideology may think of themselves as members of a winning tribe, a race of masters, and a pioneer corps of an inevitable historical process. But those who adhere to artificial right-wing ideologies are missing the depths of the realm of human affairs in their desire to force a simple explanation on it.[27]

---

and the opposition's attempt to persuade him to defect from the so-called "change government"—"to collapse it from within" in Netanyahu's words—is a good example of the detachment of the parties from their electorate in the representative system. In general, Israel is sinking into growing chaos when it comes to managing infrastructure and public service that enable the existence of a quality of life. For example, congestion on the roads, waiting for service in a government office, congestion in the education system or an appointment for medical treatment.

25. Arendt, *Crises of the Republic*, 191.

26. In this respect, the *ultra-orthodox establishment*, who naturally belongs to the bloc of loyal right-wing de-factualization agents alongside the *religious Zionism* and *peripheral Mizrachi*, is traditionally equipped with an excellent theological terminological ammunition depot for de-factualization, e.g., interpretation of the secular Zionist public as the "horde," "Gentiles who speak Hebrew," and the like.

27. Netanyahu's hard-core supporters seem to be trapped in a typical

I hope that by presenting Arendt talking about politics, my "real analysis of the existing situation" will provide the reader a perspective from which he can see that what we call "politics" today is actually a big miss, and what he thought of freedom is a necessity, the pursuit of unsatisfactory lusts, similar to addiction. Power does not give itself power, as Arendt explains. That is, government authority does not reside inside it, but it is in the people's best interests to support it. Concerning the appointment of a government, an agreement exists solely between citizens and themselves. If there is such a thing as a people-government agreement, it will be defined as the people's willingness to pay elected officials to work for them, and the elected officials' willingness to be employed by the people. The government does not have any rights. Instead, it has responsibilities. "What is to be done?" Arendt does not merely ask individuals to be more "responsible," but also for actual methods to keep powerful and dangerous people out of power. According to Arendt, a scenario in which the government transforms into a privileged club of autonomous experts who have isolated themselves from society will not change on its own. As a result, the citizens's sole remaining power is revolt. Arendt inspires future Israeli revolutionaries to start something new, namely, to generate power outside of parliament (small councils with self-government) that will significantly oppose politicians with authoritarian tendencies, bureaucratization disease, distortion of representation, governmental centralization, education system impotence, and all of this in a state of violence and the behaviorism of a mass society that backs the king over the republic, and the absence of a constitution that would protect civil disobedience.

---

ideological approach whereby there is only one way of thinking about things, which "explains everything": the Likud party is "always right," and anyone who disagrees with this loses the right to exist. However, for this reason, Gadi Yatziv rejected the definition of "post-Zionist Mizrachi," because after all, this public holds a certain kind of Zionism.

Bibliography

Arendt, Hannah. *Between Past and Future: Eight Exercises in Political Thought.* New York: Penguin, 2006.

———. *Crises of the Republic.* Harmondsworth, UK: Penguin, 1973.

———. *Eichmann in Jerusalem: A Report on the Banality of Evil.* New York: Penguin, 2006.

———. *The Human Condition.* New York: Doubleday Anchor, 1959.

———. *Jewish Writings.* Edited by Jerome Kohn and Ron H. Feldman. New York: Schocken, 2007.

———. *The Life of the Mind.* New York: Harcourt, 1981.

———. *Men in Dark Times.* New York: Harcourt, 1983.

———. *On Revolution.* London: Faber & Faber, 2016.

———. *The Origins of Totalitarianism.* New York: Schocken, 2004.

———. "Zionism Reconsidered." *Menorah Journal* 33 (1945) 162–96.

———, and Karl Jaspers. *Hannah Arendt-Karl Jaspers: Correspondence, 1926–1969.* Edited by Lotte Koehler and Hans Saner. Translated by Robert and Rita Kimber. New York: Harcourt Brace Jovanovich, 1992.

Aristotle. *Politics.* Translated by Benjamin Jowett. New York: Random House, 1943.

Clausewitz, Carl von. *On War.* Edited and translated by Michael Howard and Peter Paret. Princeton, NJ: Princeton University Press, 1976.

Dahl, Robert A. *How Democratic Is the American Constitution?* 2nd ed. New Haven, CT: Yale University Press, 2003.

Habermas, Jürgen. *Public Sphere: An Inquiry into a Category of Bourgeois Society.* Translated by Thomas Burger. Cambridge, MA: MIT Press, 1989.

Kohn, Jerome, ed. *Essays in Understanding 1930–1954.* New York: Harcourt Brace, 1994.

———. *The Promise of Politics.* New York: Schocken, 2005.

Lenin, Vladimir Ilyich. *What Is To Be Done? Burning Questions of Our Movement.* Edited by Victor J. Jerome. Translated by Joe Fineberg and George Hanna. New York: International, 1969.

Marcuse, Herbert. *Counter-Revolution and Revolt.* Boston: Beacon, 1972.

———. *An Essay on Liberation.* Boston: Beacon, 1969.

―――. *Five Lectures: Psychoanalysis, Politics, and Utopia.* Translated by Jeremy Shapiro and Shierry Weber. Boston: Beacon, 1970.

Montesquieu. *De l'Esprit des Lois* [The spirit of the laws]. Paris: Garnier Fräres, 1961.

Paine, Thomas. *Rights of Man.* Harmondsworth, UK: Penguin, 1969.

Plato. *The Dialogues of Plato.* 4 vols. Translated by R. E. Allen. New Haven, CT: Yale University Press, 1984.

Renan, Ernest. *What Is a Nation?* Translated by Ethan Rundell. Paris: Pocket, 1992.

Sartre, Jean-Paul. "Preface." In *The Wretched of the Earth*, by Fritz Fanon, translated by Constance Farrington, 7–31. New York: Grove, 1963. https://monoskop.org/images/6/6b/Fanon_Frantz_The_Wretched_of_the_Earth_1963.pdf.

Schlesinger, Arthur. *The Crisis of Confidence: Ideas, Power and Violence in America.* Boston: Houghton Mifflin, 1969.

Schmidt, Christoph, and Avner Greenberg. "The Israel of the Spirit: The German Student Movement of the 1960s and Its Attitude to the Holocaust." *Dapim: Studies on the Holocaust* 24 (Aug. 2013) 269–318. https://www.tandfonline.com/doi/abs/10.1080/23256249.2010.10744403.

Schumpeter, Joseph A. *Capitalism, Socialism and Democracy.* 3rd ed. New York: Harper Perennial Modern Thought, 2008.

Sheehan, Neil, et al. *The Pentagon Papers: As Published by the* New York Times. New York: Bantam, 1971.

Sorrell, George. *Reflections on Violence.* New York: Dover, 2005.

Stavins, Ralph, et al. *Washington Plans an Agressive War.* New York: Random House, 1971.

Tocqueville, Alexis de. *Democracy in America.* Translated by Henry Reeve. Electronic Classics Series. University Park: Pennsylvania State University Press, 2002.

Villa, Dana R. *Arendt and Heidegger: The Fate of the Political.* Princeton, NJ: Princeton University Press, 1996.

Wiker, Benjamin. *10 Books Every Conservative Must Read, Plus Four Not to Miss and One Imposter.* Washington, DC: Regnery, 2010.

Yatziv, Gadi. *Ha-hevra ha-Sektori'alit* [Sectoral society]. Jerusalem: Mosad Byalik, 1999.